D1029375

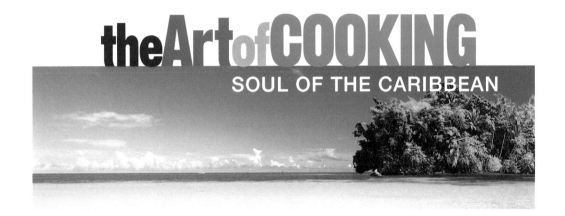

the Art of COOKING
SOUL OF THE CARIBBEAN

Selwyn Richards

minna PRESS

Copyright ©2013 Selwyn Richards

All rights reserved. This book or any portion thereof may not be reproduced or used in any manner whatsoever without the express written permission of the publisher except for the use of brief quotations in a book review.

First Printing, 2014

ISBN 978-976-95510-9-1

NATIONAL LIBRARY OF JAMAICA CATALOGUING-IN-PUBLICATION DATA
Richards, Selwyn
    The art of cooking: Soul of the Caribbean / Selwyn Richards
    p.; cm.

ISBN 978-976-95510-9-1 (pbk)
1. Cookery, Caribbean   I. Title
641.59729   dc 23

Published by Minna Press
204 Mountain View Avenue
Kingston 6, Jamaica
www.minnapress.com

Executive Editor: Lena Joy Rose

Photographer: Dalmore Sutherland

Designer: Mark Steven Weinberger

Printed in the U.S.A.

Ordering Information:
Quantity sales. Special discounts are available on quantity purchases by corporations, associations, and others.
For details, contact the publisher at:
orders@minnapress.com

SHRIMP SHOOTERS WITH VANILLA CHAI AND GREEN APPLES.
MANGO AND MIXED BERRIES

This book is dedicated
to my mother
Shela McLeod Skinner
for her inspiration and
unconditional love
and support.

...and to Caribbean people
throughout the diaspora
for keeping this vibrant cuisine
at the centre stage
of our lives.

COURTESY BELIZE TOURISM BOARD

Chef Selwyn Richards with:

(LEFT) Stephen Harper, Prime Minister of Canada

(BELOW) Brothers Travis (AT LEFT) and Lennox (AT RIGHT)

(BOTTOM) Portia Miller Simpson, Prime Minister of Jamaica.

First I must thank God for all his blessings and favour.

I am grateful to the people who have nurtured me along my culinary journey, and to my wonderful clients for their loyalty and support throughout the years.

I would like to thank The Art of Catering team—my Brothers Lennox Richards and Travis Richards, who are truly the definition of brothers—all for one and one for all. They have been by my side through thick and thin.

To my Mother, Shela McLeod Skinner, continue to wear your halo with that most infectious and radiant smile. You taught me to be passionate in everything I do. Today I stand tall because of all that you have poured into me.

To my kids, Simone Sienna Richards, Selwyn Ritché Richards and Rochon James Richards; I am so proud of the woman and men that you have become. Know that you're my heart and you have in you all the tools that you need to succeed in this life.

I would also like to acknowledge many people for their contributions and encouragement in regards to the completion of this book.

Thanks to Jennifer Hazlett, my trusted and insightful Marketing Specialist, who worked tirelessly in getting manuscript to publisher.

I am grateful to my Assistant, Laurie Rank, for providing the cottage for the photo shoot.

Much appreciation to Lucky Lankage, President of GraceKennedy in Canada; Ricardo Bryan, Vice President Sales and Marketing for Grace Canada; and Stefan Atton, Marketing Manager for GraceKennedy (Ontario) Inc., for their patronage.

I would like to thank Lena Rose, from Minna Press, for helping me in the process of editing and publishing; Justice Michael Tulloch for writing the foreword; Dalmore Sutherland, my talented photographer, for capturing the essence of my food; Fitzroy Gordon, G98.7fm President; Chef Nigel Shute my mentor; Philip Rose, Regional Director Canada, Jamaica Tourist Board; Marsha Brown and Pastor Granville Skinner for your support and prayers; my nephews for keeping the legacy alive; and Thora Daley of Thora's Elegant Design.

Finally, to Stephen Levitt, Property Master; Senator Don Meredith; Judge Pamela Appelt; Margaret Best, Former MPP of Ontario; Justice Donald McLeod—all keepers of the faith.

CYCLING IN THE BLUE MOUNTAINS. COURTESY JAMAICA TOURIST BOARD

CONTENTS

CONTENTS

CONTENTS

VIEW OF GROS PITON, COURTESY ST. LUCIA TOURIST BOARD

Selwyn Richards is a chef extraordinaire—whose taste, senses, creativity, and culinary skills have perfected Caribbean cuisine into an art which is hard to replicate.

Like most great artists, impersonators will always try to replicate their masterpieces, but only the artists himself can duplicate his originals with his own inimitable uniqueness, taste and flavour. This is what Chef Selwyn Richards has been able to achieve in his new book *The Art of Cooking: Soul of the Caribbean*. The recipes within this book both capture the flavour of the Caribbean as well as the warmth, rare spices, exotic mix and the essence of the Caribbean soul.

I have known Selwyn for over 20 years, and my family and I have had the good fortune to enjoy and benefit from his culinary skills and creativity.

In my view—with Selwyn's passion for food—his unique sense of taste, his encyclopaedic knowledge of spices and his attention to detail in food preparation, he has perfected the art of cooking. His high standards have been aptly reflected in the book.

Selwyn is one of the finest chefs and one of the most loyal and passionate ambassadors of Caribbean herbs, spices and delicacies. With *The Art of Cooking*, he has now made available to all households his unique blend of herbs and spices, as well as his simple yet creative recipes of Caribbean cuisine to North America. The book is detailed, yet easy to read, and will be a welcome addition and a mainstay in every kitchen.

The Honourable Justice Michael H. Tulloch
Ontario Court of Appeal
Canada

RAFTING ON THE RIO GRANDE, COURTESY JAMAICA TOURIST BOARD

Umami is described as the *fifth taste*. Ask most people and they'll tell you the human tongue can detect four basic tastes—sweet, sour, bitter & salty—but the sense of taste is actually much more complicated.

In recent years, Umami has been recognized as the fifth taste that involves all the senses and is said to have a spiritual or mystical quality. It evokes a special emotional response when that taste is experienced.

This special collection, *The Art of Cooking: Soul of the Caribbean*, evokes umami—memories, nostalgia, good times. Along with the classic recipes, I share my thoughts on food as well as a mélange of mouth-watering dishes from many Caribbean islands. I hope these dishes will tantalize your senses.

The Caribbean Islands produce some of the most exotic fruits and vegetables anywhere in the world. Now bring the taste of the Caribbean to your own kitchen, wherever you are. These foods and spices can be found in most local supermarkets, international stores or specialty shops. I will take you on a tour of the Caribbean; from spicy jerk chicken, escoveitch of red snapper filet, succulent curried conch and braised oxtail to pepperpot soup.

As we begin this culinary journey, with over 60 recipes and vibrant photographs, open your mind and let your senses guide you. I promise you will experience a cultural infusion of taste that is an exuberant celebration of who we are as a people.

Chef/Author

NOTHING WOULD BE MORE TIRESOME THAN EATING AND DRINKING IF GOD HAD NOT MADE THEM A PLEASURE AS WELL AS A NECESSITY.
~VOLTAIRE

Sweet
Sour
Bitter
Salty
Umami

Selwyn Richards is the Executive Chef and President of the Art of Catering, taking pride in creating enticing presentations of healthy, flavourful foods for the multicultural community. He can be contacted at: catering@theartofcatering.com or 905-619-1059, website: www.theartofcatering.com

Caribbean All-time Favourites

JAMAICA BLUE MOUNTAIN COFFEE BEANS, COURTESY JAMAICA TOURIST BOARD

Cuisine served in the Caribbean islands has been influenced by many cultures around the world. Here is a brief history.

The Food of Our Fathers

MIGRATION — CULTURAL INFLUENCES ON THE CUISINE

Caribbean cooking is rich with flavours of Africa, India and China along with Spanish, Danish, Portuguese, French and British. The genius is that each island adds its own special flavour and cooking technique. The next time you're seeking a unique dining experience, why not seek out a Caribbean restaurant? You might just discover foods that are spiced, cooked and presented differently.

RECIPES — EVOLUTION AND MODERNIZATION

African cuisine, formerly not well known in the West, has been growing in popularity as immigrants bring the dishes of their country to small family-run restaurants.

The African taste and use of ingredients has changed a great deal since intercontinental trade started on a large scale. Historically, the most important vegetable food staples were rice, sorghum, millet, barley and lentils.

As a chef, I continue to push the boundaries fusing my native cuisine with world class presentation and exotic flair.

AFRO-CARIBBEAN FOODS

The continent of Africa is the second largest land mass on Earth and is home to hundreds of different cultures and ethnic groups. African cuisine is diverse with many local culinary traditions in terms of choice of ingredients and ethnic groups.

IF THE DIVINE CREATOR HAS TAKEN PAINS TO GIVE US DELICIOUS AND EXQUISITE THINGS TO EAT, THE LEAST WE CAN DO IS PREPARE THEM WELL AND SERVE THEM WITH CEREMONY.
~ERICA EISDORFER

The same diversity exists in the Caribbean Islands. We find that many food items indigenous to the African continent are widely used all over North America, Europe and the Caribbean.

FOODS — AFRICAN AND CARIBBEAN FOODS IN THE DIASPORA

ACKEE

Ackee is native to West Africa. The island of Jamaica is the only country to have claimed the fruit and elevated it to a premier exotic dish.

BREADFRUIT

Breadfruit is a vegetable that can be eaten roasted, fried or boiled.

CALLALOO

It's the name given to the leaves of a variety of plants such as taro (dasheen). It is often used to make soup. The soup includes numerous other ingredients such as crab or pig's tail, okra and hot peppers. Similar to spinach, the leaves can also be cooked and served as a vegetable.

CASSAVA

Cassava was a mainstay of Jamaica's indigenous people, the Tainos. Today, the grated cassava is made into a flatbread and deep-fried as a savory side-dish. It's a great accompaniment to spicy foods like jerk pork or escoveitch fish. Casareep is the juice of the cassava root which is flavoured with aromatics and boiled to remove the toxins. It is used as a relish in pepperpot and other dishes. Casareep is also used to preserve meat in tropical countries.

COCONUT

Coconut palms are grown throughout the tropics for decoration as well as for their many culinary and non-culinary uses; virtually every part of the coconut palm has some use. The "nut" of the coconut is edible and is located on the inner surface of the shell. The juice of the coconut can be

refreshing to drink. The oil from the coconut has moisturizing and healing properties.

FISH

Fish plays a major role in the diet of most Africans throughout the diaspora. Because of the proximity to great bodies of water, fresh fish and seafood are readily available.

FUFU

Fufu is a traditional dish that is made by boiling starchy foods such as cassava, yam, plantain or rice. The fufu is then pounded into a glutinous mass resulting in one of West Africa's favourite dishes. This dish is enjoyed in many Caribbean islands such as Cuba, Puerto Rico and the Dominican Republic.

GOAT

Curried goat, or goat curry (depending on which island you're on), takes on the same importance as Boer Goat Suya, native to South Africa. (Suya: African shish kebabs that consist of roasted meat coated with a spicy peanut rub; fiery and aromatic). On many islands, curried goat is a staple dish at special occasions such as funerals, weddings, dances and other events.

MANGO

Mango is a fruit which comes in many varieties, sizes, tastes and colours. When ripe, the flesh is yellow and sweet and can be eaten raw or cooked. Green mangos are used to make some of the best chutneys and vegetable stews.

PLANTAINS

The plantain is a staple across Africa and the Caribbean. It is a larger version of the banana, and must be cooked to be edible. Green or ripe plantains are sliced, fried, boiled or baked before eaten.

YAMS

Yam is a tuber and is served boiled, mashed or roasted. Pounded yam comes in countless varieties and is the main staple in many parts of Africa.

SUYA SPICE

African shish kebabs are called suya, consisting of roasted meat coated with a spicy peanut rub. Throughout West Africa, suya street vendors are a common sight in both the cities and villages. You can find them grilling skewered meat over open pits from late morning until after midnight. Beef is the most common suya, although chicken and veal are also popular.

INGREDIENTS

2 pounds of beef, chicken or veal

Finely ground roasted peanuts

Cayenne pepper to taste

Paprika to taste

Salt to taste

Ground ginger to taste

Onion powder to taste

METHOD

1. Shell fresh peanuts and place them on a shallow baking sheet.
2. Roast for 20 to 25 minutes in a 350°F oven.
3. Cool the peanuts between layers of paper towels to remove any excess oil.
4. Grind the cooled roasted peanuts into a powder. Use a mortar and pestle, or place the peanuts in a plastic bag and crush them with a rolling pin, or use a food processor.
5. Squeeze the ground peanuts in a paper towel for one or two minutes to remove excess oil.
6. Put the peanut powder in a mixing bowl.
7. Add the other spices to taste.
8. Add more cayenne pepper for a spicier suya.
9. Leave out the cayenne pepper and add more paprika for a milder suya.
10. Mix the spices thoroughly.
11. Divide the spice mixture in half.
12. Cut two pounds of meat into bite-sized chunks.
13. Roll the meat into the suya until it is coated on all sides.
14. Let the coated meat rest for 30 minutes so that the spices can permeate.
15. Start the grill or preheat the broiler.
16. Place the meat on skewers.
17. Alternate with pieces of onion, green and red pepper and plum tomato.
18. Cook the meat until done. Make sure that chicken is cooked thoroughly.
19. Serve the meat with the reserved half of the suya.

SERVES 6-8

Chicken is routinely eaten at evening mealtime in North American households. We each have our favourite ways of preparing it. When cooking a whole chicken, you can do wonders with the leftovers.

Seven Ways to Stretch that Chicken and Make it Go Further

1. The skeleton of the chicken can be used to create a broth. Learn to slice a whole chicken. Slicing one properly makes it easier to remove the rest of the meat from the bone. Place the slices aside and boil what's left in some water until the rest of the meat falls off the bone. You can season the broth with herbs and spices. After it cools, pour it into jars for storage. You'll be able to keep the broth for a few weeks. Use it to flavour soups and casseroles.

2. Instead of buying luncheon meat, slice leftover chicken breast for sandwiches. It will be a nice change from the usual lunch fare.

3. Cube a few pieces to toss on top of a salad with some cheese and croutons.

4. Combine with peppers and onions in a skillet to make filling for fajitas or soft tacos. On the weekends, instead of ordering a pizza or going to McDonald's, use that chicken.

5. Does your family like chicken pot pie? Add some of that chicken, along with vegetables (canned or frozen) and a can of creamed soup to a pie crust and you've got an instant dinner that takes less than an hour to prepare. It is a quick meal idea perfect for busy families. A salad on the side will make a complete and healthy dinner.

6. Chicken-based casseroles can be made and frozen for future meals. The family may be all "chickened out" for the week, but that doesn't mean you can't make the most of the chicken you have left for future weeks.

7. Do you still have more chicken? Well let's keep going with more ideas. Hey, our mothers and grandmothers learned to use chicken in many ways and so can we. What tastes the best when you have a cold and are feeling under the weather? Why, chicken noodle soup of course. Don't settle for canned soup with small noodles. Make your own soup with juicy chicken pieces and wide egg noodles. That broth you stored in the refrigerator will serve as a nice base and best of all it is already seasoned. Add wide egg noodles and sliced vegetables like carrots, celery, and onions to your soup. When the noodles are tender, add the chicken. Since it is already cooked, it just needs warming. Ladle up a bowl for the sick and the healthy as a light weekend lunch.

What are you doing with your chicken after dinner tonight? Try some of these ideas to make that chicken do double and triple duty to save on your family's grocery bill. The best part is that the new meals are just as tasty and healthy as the original dish.

BONELESS JERK CHICKEN

When we talk about Jamaican cuisine, the first thing that comes to mind is Jerk Chicken—a style of barbecue that is native to Jamaica. In most upscale kitchens in North America you will find Grace® Jerk Seasoning along with many different island spices. Chefs from all over Europe and North America have been trending towards fusing this tropical island paradise cuisine on their menu. The chicken, pork, fish, or shellfish is marinated with the spicy mixture called Jamaican jerk sauce. What better way to add some heat to a long winter than enjoying some Jerk Chicken with friends and fantasizing about lying on a beach in Ocho Rios?

INGREDIENTS

- 6 boneless chicken breasts or thighs
- 3 tablespoons Grace Jerk Seasoning
- 2 tablespoons tomato ketchup
- 1 teaspoon chopped garlic
- 1 teaspoon chopped thyme
- 1 teaspoon salt
- 1 teaspoon black pepper
- 2 tablespoons soy sauce
- 3 tablespoons vegetable oil

METHOD

1. Combine all ingredients together in a bowl, mix well and marinate in fridge from 4 to 24 hours.
2. Bake chicken in oven at 375°F for 30 minutes, turning once.
3. Chicken can also be cooked on the grill with medium heat, turning often until done.
4. Serve chicken with rice and peas.

SERVES 6

SELWYN'S TIP

*Marinating is the key for this recipe—
the longer time,
the deeper flavour of jerk*

CURRY CHICKEN

Curry stew chicken is a hearty meal that is enjoyed by many in the diaspora for a quick and easy taste of home.

INGREDIENTS

- 6 tablespoons of Grace Curry Powder
- 1½ tablespoons of vegetable oil
- 1 onion
- 3 stalks scallion
- 5 sprigs fresh thyme
- 4 cloves garlic, chopped
- 1 hot pepper (ideally Scotch bonnet)
- 2 teaspoon salt
- 2 teaspoon pepper
- 2 teaspoon Grace All Purpose Seasoning
- 1 whole or boneless chicken (about 2½ - 3 pounds)
- 2 potatoes
- 2 cups water
- 1 cup Grace Coconut Milk

METHOD

1. Cut the chicken in small pieces.
2. Dice the onion, scallion, pepper and garlic into small pieces.
3. Rub all of the ingredients (except the last three) into the chicken and allow to marinate in the refrigerator for up to two hours.
4. Cube the potato into 1-inch pieces.
5. Sauté the chicken (5 to 10 minutes).
6. Add the potatoes, Grace Coconut Milk and water to the pan, cover and simmer until the sauce has a thick consistency (about ½ hour).

Serve with Festival or Rice and Peas.

SERVES 6

SELWYN'S TIP

*You can mix a packet of Grace Coconut Milk Powder
to one cup of water to get one cup of coconut milk*

JAMAICAN RICE AND PEAS

This is the traditional Sunday staple side dish that's enjoyed with braised oxtail, cook-down chicken or any entrée.

INGREDIENTS

1½ cups cooked red kidney beans, liquid reserved

2 cloves garlic, chopped

1¼ cups Grace Coconut Milk

1 cup water

1 cup rice

2 stalks of scallion, crushed

1 or 2 sprigs fresh thyme

Salt to taste

Coarse black pepper to taste

METHOD

1. Cook red kidney beans to package directions. Reserve bean liquid.
2. Place cooked beans into a large saucepan or pot.
3. Add chopped garlic.
4. Measure all liquids, including reserved bean liquid, Grace Coconut Milk and water; enough to make 2¼ cups.
5. Add the 2¼ cups of liquid to the beans and garlic in the pot.
6. Add rice, crushed scallion, thyme, salt and pepper to taste.
7. Bring to a boil.
8. Reduce heat.
9. Cover and cook for about 20 minutes or until all liquid is absorbed.

SERVES 4

CURRY TOFU WITH PORTOBELLO MUSHROOM

Who says one has to eat meat for a Caribbean taste? This recipe is a vegetarian's delight with all the flavours of home.

INGREDIENTS

¼ cup sweet onion, diced

1 teaspoon olive oil

2 tablespoons Grace Curry Powder

½ cup Grace Coconut Milk

½ cup firm or specialty tofu

1 large Portobello mushroom, cleaned

Fresh parsley or cilantro (garnish), chopped

1 small eggplant, diced

1 teaspoon Grace All Purpose Seasoning

METHOD

1. Sauté onion and curry powder with oil over medium-low heat until onion is soft and translucent for 2 to 3 minutes.

2. Add eggplant, sliced mushroom, tofu and Grace Coconut Milk.

3. Add salt and pepper to taste and simmer for about 5 minutes.

Serve with steamed jasmine rice.

SERVES 4

BBQ PORK WITH JERK MARINADE AND TAMARIND CHUTNEY

2 pounds pork loin or pork chops (½ pound a person)

3 tablespoons Grace Jerk Seasoning

2 tablespoons tomato ketchup

1 teaspoon chopped garlic

1 teaspoon chopped thyme

1 teaspoon salt

1 teaspoon black pepper

2 tablespoons soy sauce

3 tablespoons vegetable oil

1 teaspoon sugar

Jar of tamarind chutney

METHOD

1. Combine all ingredients together in a bowl, mix well and let marinate in fridge from 4 to 24 hours.
2. Cook pork in oven at 375°F for 30 minutes, turning once.
3. Pork can also be cooked on the grill with medium heat, turning often until done.

Serve with Tamarind Chutney.

SERVES 4

BRAISED OXTAIL WITH GRACE LIMA BEANS

This is a popular dish on many Caribbean islands and each island has its own unique touch. Here's a classic recipe.

INGREDIENTS

- 2 pounds sliced oxtail
- 2 tablespoons vegetable oil
- 1 tablespoon salt
- 2 tablespoons soy sauce
- 2 tablespoons Grace All Purpose Seasoning
- 1 tablespoon paprika
- 1 tablespoon black pepper
- 2 medium onions, diced
- 1 clove garlic, chopped
- 4 medium carrots, diced
- 1 litre water or beef stock
- 2 stalks scallion
- 1 sprig thyme
- 2 cans Grace Lima Beans

METHOD

1. Season oxtail with soy sauce, seasoning, paprika, garlic and salt & pepper.
2. Marinate in refrigerator for at least 1 hour.
3. Heat oven to 375°F.
4. Place meat in deep roasting pan in oven for ½ hour, turning a few times.
5. Add water or stock, thyme, onions and cook for a further 1½ hours.
6. Adjust seasoning with salt and pepper.
7. Add carrots and beans, stir well.
8. Cover with foil or roasting pan lid and simmer for another hour or until meat is falling off the bone tender.
9. Serve hot with rice and peas.

Serves 4

PAN FRY CHICKEN BREASTS

This is an updated, healthier version of an old favourite . Chicken breasts need to be handled delicately to keep it moist. This recipe is a simple preparation but is extremely tasty by pan frying (not deep frying) or searing and baking in the oven.

INGREDIENTS

    4 boneless, skinless chicken breasts

    1 cup seasoning flour

    2 tablespoons Grace All Purpose Seasoning

    ½ cup vegetable oil

METHOD

1. Heat a skillet or frying pan over medium heat.
2. Dredge seasoned chicken breasts in flour shaking off excess flour.
3. Place in pan for two minutes on each side then bake in 350°F preheated oven for 15 minutes.

Serve with sautéed spinach or collard greens and roasted candied yams.

SERVES 4

ROTI

Roti is the taco or burrito of the Caribbean. With its origins in India, roti is eaten throughout the Caribbean and is a popular mainstay of Trinidad's cuisine. It's a flatbread that is used to soak up the sauce of various curry dishes such as goat, chicken, beef, shrimp or non-meat dishes. These meats also provide a delicious filling for the roti.

INGREDIENTS

> 2 cups whole wheat flour (chapati flour)
>
> ½ teaspoon salt (optional)
>
> 4 teaspoons oil
>
> ¾ cup warm water
>
> All-purpose flour, for rolling and dusting

METHOD

1. In a large mixing bowl, mix chapati flour and salt well.
2. Add oil and mix until all lumps are gone.
3. Add warm water a little at a time to form a medium soft dough ball. Do not overwork the dough.
4. Add few drops of oil and coat the dough ball.
5. Cover and let it rest for 15 minutes.
6. Heat tawa or skillet over medium heat.
7. Knead the dough once and divide into golf ball size balls.
8. Dip one ball into the all-purpose flour to coat and roll it out into a thin disc.
9. Keep dipping the roti into the dry flour to prevent it from sticking to the rolling surface.
10. Shake or rub off excess flour from the roti and place it onto the hot tawa.
11. Flip to the other side once you see bubbles appear on the surface.
12. Allow it to cook for 10 to 15 seconds.
13. Increase the stove heat to high, gently pick the roti up with tongs, remove the tawa from the flame, flip the roti over and place onto an open flame.
14. The roti should balloon up.
15. Flip it over and cook on the other side.
16. Place the cooked roti into an insulated container and smear it with Ghee or clarified butter and repeat the process for the remaining dough.
17. Makes approximately 12 rotis.

SELWYN'S TIP

Make large batches of roti and freeze some in small freezer Ziploc bags. The trick is not to add oil, Ghee or butter before freezing. Simply reheat the roti on a hot tawa then add your oil

FESTIVAL DUMPLINGS

As a kid I spent many a weekend on Hellshire beach, just outside of Kingston, Jamaica. This is without a doubt where festival was invented. The fishermen would pull their boats right up on the beach where you could see all the ladies in their aprons running to buy fish that had just been caught. Within thirty minutes, the women would clean and prepare the fish for frying. While waiting for the fishermen to return to shore, the ladies came up with the idea of making festivals as hors d'oeuvres for the beachgoers. As kids, we enjoyed the fresh fried dumplings more than the fish. Looking back now, these are all the magical moments that shape my career as a chef.

INGREDIENTS

- 1 cup cornmeal
- 1 cup corn flour
- 1 cup all-purpose flour
- ½ cup sugar
- ½ teaspoon salt
- 2 tablespoons baking power
- ½ cup orange juice
- 1 cup water
- 3 cups vegetable oil

METHOD

1. Mix all the dry ingredients in a medium size bowl.
2. Add orange juice and water to make dough.
3. Make dough into little balls, twisted or ovals.
4. Heat oil in a heavy fry pan or Dutch pot until very hot, around 300°F, be careful not to overheat oil.
5. Gently put dough in hot oil a few at a time.
6. Deep fry until golden brown.

SERVES 6

FRY BAKES

Fry Bakes are to Trinidadians what Festival is to Jamaicans.

INGREDIENTS

2 cups flour

2 teaspoons baking powder

1 teaspoon salt

½ cup butter

1 teaspoon sugar

Water

Vegetable oil for frying

METHOD

1. Sift together the flour, baking powder, and salt.
2. Add the shortening and sugar, and mix with a fork.
3. Add enough water to make a dough and knead gently.
4. Cut the dough into 4 to 6 pieces (depending on how large you want the bakes to be) and roll each piece into a ball.
5. Let stand for a few minutes.
6. Flatten the balls of dough until they are about ¼-inch thick, and fry in hot oil until they are brown.
7. Remove and drain on paper towels.

SERVES 6

MOM'S CURRY GOAT

My mom is a great cook who loves to entertain. While I was growing up, my home was one big revolving door of people stopping by for Saturday soup and Sunday dinners. This is one of mom's recipes that I'm sure you'll enjoy.

INGREDIENTS

- 4 pounds goat leg or shoulder cut into 2-inch chunks
- 8 tablespoons Grace Curry Powder
- ½ cup vegetable oil
- 1 large onion, chopped
- 1 tablespoon fresh ginger root, chopped
- 4 cloves of garlic, mashed
- 1 Scotch bonnet pepper, whole
- 12 whole pimento berries
- 5 tablespoons Grace All Purpose Seasoning
- 2 teaspoons salt
- 2 teaspoons ground black pepper
- 1 teaspoon Grace Jerk Seasoning
- 1 bunch fresh thyme, chopped
- 6 cups water
- 3 Yukon gold potatoes, peeled and cubed (optional)

METHOD

1. Rinse goat meat thoroughly, pat dry with paper towel and place in large bowl.
2. Add Grace Curry Powder, Grace All Purpose Seasoning, fresh ginger, 1 tablespoon of vegetable oil, salt and pepper.
3. Mix and wrap with plastic wrap, marinate for at least 4 hours.
4. In a Dutch or crock pot heat oil, add meat and sauté until all the meat is brown, add onion, ½ of the chopped thyme and garlic.
5. Sauté for another 5 minutes stirring constantly so meat does not burn.
6. Add water, Scotch bonnet pepper, pimento berries, jerk seasoning and bring to a boil.
7. Reduce heat to low and simmer for 2½ hours or until fork tender, stirring occasionally. Just before serving, add remaining chopped thyme.
8. Curry goat can be served with steamed rice or rice and peas.

SERVES 8

SELWYN'S TIP

If you are pressed for time, you can use a pressure cooker and cut your cooking time in half

CONCH FRITTER

There is no island that loves conch like the Bahamas. Conch is curried, fried, ceviche, made into a salad or is the main flavor in conch soup. Conch fritter is a great hors d'oeuvre by itself or with an assortment of dips.

INGREDIENTS

    1 pound conch meat, 1-inch cubes

    1 tablespoon lemon juice

    1 teaspoon cayenne pepper (or Scotch bonnet pepper sauce)

    1 teaspoon salt

    Pinch ground pepper

    1 teaspoon fresh thyme (chopped)

    2 stalks fresh green onion (scallion chopped)

    2 cups flour

    1 tablespoon baking power

    1 cup cold water

    4 cups vegetable oil (for deep frying)

METHOD

1. In a medium bowl add diced conch, lemon juice, cayenne pepper, salt, pepper, thyme and scallions and mix thoroughly.
2. Wrap with plastic and let marinate in fridge for ½ hour.
3. In another bowl, add flour, baking powder and water.
4. Mix into a batter.
5. Add marinated conch to batter, mix well.
6. In deep fry pan, heat oil over medium heat.
7. Spoon batter with conch pieces into hot oil, they should each form a nice round ball.
8. Cook until golden brown.
9. Remove from fry pan and drain on paper towel.
10. Serve hot with mango salsa.

SERVES 6

SELWYN'S TIP

Make mango salsa by simply dicing a ripe mango and tossing with diced red and green sweet peppers, jalapeno peppers, scallions and juice from one lime

CONCH AND LOBSTER CEVICHE

Antigua is no different than most of the Caribbean Islands that are experimenting with culinary fusion. With the introduction of The International Mango Festival, both local and international chefs have been pairing everything from Mango Encrusted Mahi to Mango Stuffed Lamb Loin and consequently I had the best one night trip to Sandals, Antigua! This recipe is courtesy of my good friend Erica Henry-Jackman, Director of Tourism for Antigua and Barbuda.

INGREDIENTS

2 cups cleaned and diced fresh conch (or frozen, thawed)

2 cups diced poached lobster (about 2 lobsters)

3 scallions stalks, diced

½ red pepper, diced

½ yellow pepper, diced

½ green pepper, diced

½ small pineapple, peeled and diced

2 Scotch bonnet peppers, finely chopped

½ bunch chopped fresh cilantro

½ bunch chopped fresh basil

½ bunch chopped fresh mint

1 tablespoon grated fresh ginger

Juice from ½ lime

¼ cup rice wine vinegar

½ cup extra virgin olive oil

Salt and pepper to taste

METHOD

1. In a medium bowl, combine all ingredients and mix well.
2. Season to taste.
3. Marinate for about 3 hours in refrigerator, tossing occasionally just before serving.
4. Freeze martini glasses and fill with ceviche. Serve with crispy plantain chips.

OIL DOWN - GRENADA'S NATIONAL DISH

In Grenada, being invited to an Oil Down could take on erotic connotations, however, shedding your robe is not mandatory. Instead it's a cultural experience that is unique and filling - comfort food at its very best. This one-pot meal can be flavoured with lots of different meat or fish. The key ingredients— salt beef, pig tails or salted cod, breadfruit, green figs (green bananas), callaloo and Grace Coconut Milk—release the exotic oil as it simmers.

INGREDIENTS

2 pounds salt beef

1 breadfruit

4 cups Grace Coconut Milk

7 green figs (or green bananas), peeled

1 medium onion, chopped

8 to 10 dasheen leaves or callaloo

2 medium carrots, chopped

2 sprigs fresh thyme

½ cup chives, chopped

2 garlic cloves, chopped

3 pimento peppers, seeded and chopped

2 teaspoon turmeric (saffron)

Salt and pepper to taste

METHOD

1. Place salt beef in a pot with cold water.
2. Bring to a boil and drain.
3. Repeat three times to remove preserving salt.
4. Cook until tender and drain.
5. Peel and wash breadfruit.
6. Cut into eight sections.
7. Remove center lengthwise of each section.
8. Cut into ½-inch slices.
9. Sauté onions and garlic in hot oil.
10. Add salt beef, chives, thyme, pepper, saffron and Grace Coconut Milk.
11. Add breadfruit, figs, carrots, dasheen leaves, cover pot and bring to a boil.
12. Reduce heat and simmer for about 45 minutes until breadfruit is cooked and tender.
13. Add salt and pepper to taste.

SERVES 6

MASHED GREEN BANANA SUPREME

Think of mashed potatoes, only we're using green boiled bananas piped into rosettes, or just a casserole dish with parmesan cheese sprinkled on top.

INGREDIENTS

    6 - 8 green bananas

    1 lime cut in half

    2 litres of water

    ¼ cup butter or margarine

    ¼ cup milk

    ½ cup parmesan cheese

    salt and pepper to taste

METHOD

1. In a medium pot add water and bring to a boil.
2. Cut ends off bananas, core lengthwise and add to pot.
3. Add lime and salt to taste.
4. Cook for 15 minutes or until tender.
5. Remove from heat, drain and discard the skin of the bananas.
6. In a mixing bowl at medium speed mix the bananas and butter for two minutes.
7. Add milk and parmesan cheese.
8. Add in salt and pepper to taste.
9. Spoon mixture in a piping bag and pipe donut sized rosettes on a greased baking sheet.
10. Or spoon mixture into a casserole dish with a sprinkle of parmesan cheese on top.
11. Bake at 350°F for 20 minutes.

SERVES 4

Grilling Island Style

With the arrival of summer and rising temperatures comes the fire of the Barbecue—cooking food over an open flame! Buried in a pit with coals, special woods, hanging in a hot smoker or whatever the cultural tradition is, there is no better way to gather people to celebrate than with the power of the fire.

Time to Fire up the *Grill*

TODAY WE CALL THIS PHENOMENON BARBECUE

When you discuss barbecue, you're talking family secrets, cooking equipment and oh, the sauces! With the modern backyard grills, you can prepare the entire meal—from salads and main courses to dessert.

I remember where I was when the Toronto Blue Jays became "World Series" champions. It was back when I was one of the Chefs at SkyDome in Toronto. Being a foodie, what I remember most is a player by the name of Joe Carter, flying in barbecued ribs from his friends' restaurant in Kansas City for all his team mates to enjoy after each home game. As the Chef responsible for feeding the players, I was more than upset. What? Did he think my food was not good enough? After all these years I finally understand, we are people of many cultures and nobody cooks our cultural food better than the ones we trust. Over the years I have perfected my own boneless Jerk Chicken that makes people sing in many different languages.

GRILLING SAFELY

Think about grilling safety. Are you doing the right things? And are you really safe?

The gas grill, as fun as it gets, is still a major appliance that needs maintenance and care while using. Most gas grills are fueled by liquefied petroleum gas or propane. Unburned gas accidentally released or leaking from a gas grill can cause a dangerous fire or explosion.

You should check your grill before each use, and:

- Check hoses for cracks or holes and replace any hose that appears to be damaged.
- Follow your manufacturer's instructions for checking the connection to the cylinder every time a new cylinder is connected to the grill.
- If you smell gas, turn the grill off immediately and do not use until the problem can be corrected.
- Always open the lid of a grill before igniting it.
- Do not move a grill while in use.
- Keep your grill on a flat level surface.

These are just a few tips you should keep in mind. When we're in the middle of having a good time we don't always think about these safety precautions.

CHICKEN TIPS

So you have twenty guests coming over and everyone wants your famous barbecued chicken.
Here is a little tip that, if done right, will give you amazing results.

- Wash and cut chicken into desired pieces. In a stock pot half-filled with water, add salt and pepper, chopped celery, chopped onions, carrots, thyme, garlic and your little soup secrets. Put chicken pieces in pot and simmer for fifteen minutes. You are not making soup you are blanching the chicken (pre-cooking).
- Remove chicken from liquid and place in stainless steel bowl. While chicken is hot, add your favourite type of barbecue sauce and cover. You can do this overnight or leave in fridge for a few hours. Cook chicken on grill brushing often with barbecue sauce.

Now you know for sure your chicken is well cooked without being burnt to a crisp and raw in the middle. Left-over liquid is great for boiling corn.

SCRUMPTIOUS SKEWERS

The general idea with skewers is to create a pleasing colour arrangement. Vary the ingredients up and down the skewers. Marinated boneless cubes of chicken or pork with onions, red, green and yellow peppers make great hors d'oeuvres. You can do the same with chunks of king fish or salmon. For vegetarians; zucchini, eggplants, red onions, peppers and mushrooms seasoned with fresh herbs and olive oil.

BBQ CHICKEN

INGREDIENTS

2 pounds boneless, skinless chicken

3 tablespoons mixed seasoning

2 tablespoons fresh thyme (chopped)

2 tablespoons vegetable oil

1 cup barbecue sauce

2 tablespoons chili sauce

METHOD

1. Heat grill.
2. In a shallow bowl, mix seasoning with chicken, thyme and vegetable oil.
3. Marinate in fridge for ½ hour.
4. Place chicken on grill over medium heat.
5. Add chili sauce to barbecue sauce, brush generously on chicken.
6. Cook for about 15 minutes, turning once or twice.

SERVES 4

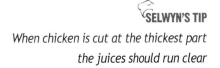

SELWYN'S TIP

When chicken is cut at the thickest part
the juices should run clear

CITRUS SUNSET JERK GROUPER

INGREDIENTS

   2 teaspoons Grace All Purpose Seasoning

   2 tablespoons Grace Jerk Seasoning

   1 cup olive oil

   1 tablespoon minced garlic

   2 teaspoons brown sugar

   ½ cup orange juice

   1 cup soy sauce

   2 pounds grouper, cut into 4 filets

METHOD

   1. Place everything except the fish in a large glass bowl and whisk together well.

   2. Add the grouper filets to the jerk marinade, cover, and put in refrigerator to marinate for anywhere from one to four hours. The longer you leave it, the more intense the flavour.

   3. Set grill heat to medium-high heat.

   4. Remove grouper from marinade and when grill is ready, put grouper on grill for 5 or 6 minutes, flip and cook for another five or six minutes or until fish is white and no longer transparent.

   5. Remove to platter and serve immediately with mashed potatoes or grilled plantain.

There's nothing like sharing food in the great outdoors to give you plenty of reasons to smile.

Grilled Picnic. Get Fired Up with Fresh Ideas

Firing up the grill for a picnic usually brings on thoughts of hamburgers, hot dogs, and barbecued chicken. That's all dandy and certainly delicious, but wouldn't you like your grilled food to stand out a little from the rest? Perhaps there are ways to present old favourites on the grill in new ways, or even try something completely different. Here are a few thoughts about new ways to grill your summertime dishes.

Fish is a grilling favourite at picnics. Use fish that is firm and solid so it grills well and doesn't fall apart or become dry. Oily fish like salmon is perfect on the grill, but there are many other types of fish that work equally well. Fish grills best when you don't have to flip it with a spatula, that's why you want to invest in a grilling basket which encloses the fish and you flip the basket instead of the fish itself.

Other seafood that's perfect picnic food for the grill is shrimp, scallops, and lobster. Shrimp can be grilled unpeeled to help keep them from overcooking. Lobster can be grilled in the shell, as well. Use a tray made for the grill with smaller slots to keep smaller seafood, like shrimp and scallops, from falling through. Marinate the seafood in a variety of flavours for a different flavour each time you have a grilling picnic.

Sometimes, you need to rethink the way you prepare your main dishes at a grilling picnic to make serving simple. Think shish-kabobs and you hardly even need to bring plates! These bite-size pieces are a great way to cook, serve, and eat your favourite foods easily at a grilling picnic. Alternately cut up meat, meat balls, poultry, or seafood with grape tomatoes, chunks of sweet onions, peppers, zucchini, yellow squash, or mushrooms. Some foods lend themselves very well to a tropical taste, too. Include pineapple chunks or citrus with chicken or seafood for a taste of the islands.

As you can see, you can grill just about anything you want to serve at your picnic. Even if you choose to serve sandwiches, why not grill them? When you fire up your grill for your picnic, don't limit the menu to hotdogs and hamburgers. Use your imagination. If you can cook it, you can grill it!

ISLAND BURGERS WITH GRILLED PINEAPPLE SALSA

INGREDIENTS

2 pounds ground beef

Salt and black pepper

Dash garlic salt

1 pineapple, peeled and sliced lengthwise

1 sweet red bell pepper, diced

⅛ cup pickled ginger, diced

⅛ cup soy sauce

⅛ cup rice wine vinegar

Hamburger buns

METHOD

1. Heat grill to medium.
2. Brush lengths of pineapple with cooking oil and place on grill.
3. Cook, turning a few times, until pineapple is hot and has good grill marks.
4. Remove to cutting board and allow to cool.
5. Cut pineapple into small pieces and put in bowl; add sweet red bell pepper, pickled ginger, soy sauce, rice wine vinegar, and salt and pepper; toss to combine, taste and adjust seasonings. Refrigerate until burgers are ready.
6. Turn grill up to high for burgers.
7. Form the beef into thick patties, season with salt, pepper, and dash of garlic powder.
8. When grill is ready, cook burgers 3 to 4 minutes, flip, then continue grilling for 3 to 4 minutes or until done as desired.
9. Serve hot burgers on hamburger buns (toasted on the grill if desired) with a large spoonful of chilled pineapple salsa.

DESSERT ON THE BBQ

You can use any firm-fleshed fruit to make colourful, quick and easy grilled kabobs.

INGREDIENTS

2 nectarines

1 mango peeled, halved and pitted

4 red plums, halved and pitted

¼ fresh pineapple

2 bananas, peeled and thickly sliced

2 kiwi fruit

3 tablespoons melted butter

2 tablespoons dark rum

1 tablespoon orange juice

4 tablespoons brown sugar

Pinch of ground cinnamon

METHOD

1. Halve and remove stones from the nectarines.
2. Cut the pieces in half again and place on a large, shallow dish.
3. Cut the mango and pineapple into chunks and add to dish with the kiwi fruits, plums and bananas.
4. Over medium heat combine the butter with the rum, sugar, orange juice and cinnamon.
5. Boil for 1 to 2 minutes, pour over fruits and mix well.
6. Marinate for 1 hour.
7. Thread the fruits on to skewers and cook on a medium grill, turning and brushing frequently with the reserved marinade.

SERVES 4

GRILLED BANANAS

As you barbecue this summer I hope you have fun preparing delicious and imaginative menus. Grab your spatula, apron and fire up those grills!

INGREDIENTS

    6 bananas

    3 tablespoons melted butter

    2 tablespoons dark rum

    1 tablespoon orange juice

    4 tablespoons brown sugar

    Pinch of ground cinnamon

METHOD

1. Over medium heat combine the butter with rum, sugar, orange juice and cinnamon.
2. Boil for 1 to 2 minutes to make marinade.
3. Slice 4 to 6 bananas (with skin on) in half, lengthwise.
4. Use a pastry brush to brush marinade on bananas.
5. Place bananas on grill, cut side down.
6. 6.Cook for about two minutes on medium heat, turn and brush for another two minutes.

This is an excellent dessert with ice cream or by itself.

Seafood—Soul of the Caribbean

ACKEE & SMOKED SALMON VAL-AU-VENT

The Great Jamaican Breakfast—Ackee!

Ackee is a fruit that is native to West Africa but is consumed mainly in Jamaican cuisine. It is a fruit and not a vegetable as most people might believe. Ackee is not only Jamaica's National Fruit, but ackee and salt fish is the National Dish. This dish is mainly served for breakfast with fried dumplings, fried plantain or with breadfruit. I am proud to say you have not had a real Jamaican breakfast until you have eaten ackee and salt fish with fried dumpling, festival or hard dough bread and a cup of freshly brewed Blue Mountain coffee. Over the years I have tried to put a different spin on my favourite ackee dish so I have substituted smoked salmon or smoked marlin and stuffed it in a pastry shell or val-au-vent shell that's made with puff pastry. It makes a great hors d'oeuvres or appetizer.

INGREDIENTS

1 can ackee or fresh, boiled	1 sprig fresh thyme, chopped
½ pound of smoked salmon (julienne)	¼ cup olive oil
1 onion diced	1 teaspoon black pepper
1 red pepper diced	Salt to taste
1 green pepper diced	2 boxes frozen tart shells (2½-inches)
1 clove garlic chopped	

METHOD

1. In a medium pot heat oil, add onions, garlic and sauté for two minutes.
2. Add peppers and smoked salmon.
3. Sauté for another two minutes then add drained ackee, thyme, pepper and salt to taste.
4. Sauté for another three minutes.
5. Bake tart shells in oven at 350°F for 20 minutes or until golden brown, careful not to overcook.
6. Let cool on rack for 15 minutes.
7. Remove from foil and add ackee to shells.

Serve with plantain, bread or festival.

STUFFED SNAPPER FILET WITH CALLALOO
AND A LIGHT COCONUT CURRY CREAM SAUCE

There are various species of red snapper, but real red snapper is a prized fish and is loved by fish connoisseurs the world over. It has a firm texture and sweet nutty flavour that can stand up to very strong spices.

INGREDIENTS

6 to 8 red snapper filets (fresh or frozen)

2 cups of fresh, sautéed or canned callaloo

1 small onion, diced

1 clove garlic, chopped

1 sprig fresh thyme, chopped

1 cup Grace Coconut Milk

½ cup fish stock (water)

3 tablespoons Grace Curry Powder

Salt

Black pepper

½ teaspoon paprika

¼ cup olive oil

METHOD

1. Make sure filets are dry, season with salt, pepper and paprika, cover and leave in refrigerator for 15 minutes.
2. Lay your filet flat on the counter.
3. At one end put a bit of seasoned callaloo and roll into a roulade.
4. Grease a baking tray and stand roulade upright.
5. Use a tooth pick to hold it together if falling apart.
6. Drizzle half of the olive oil over filet.
7. Bake in oven on broil for 15 minutes.

SAUCE:

1. In a sauce pan on medium heat add the remaining oil, onions, garlic and Grace Curry Powder.
2. Sauté for 2 minutes.
3. Add fish stock, Grace Coconut Milk, thyme, salt and pepper to taste and simmer for 5 minutes on low heat.

Serve with sautéed vegetables, rosette of mashed green banana supreme or with mashed potatoes

ESCOVEITCH OF RED SNAPPER

INGREDIENTS FOR FISH

3 pounds red snapper or fish of your choice

2 or 3 limes

½ cup flour

2 teaspoons salt

2 teaspoons garlic powder

2 teaspoons black pepper

About ½ cup oil for frying

1 tablespoon unsalted butter

INGREDIENTS FOR SAUCE

1 tablespoon oil

2 or 3 Scotch bonnet peppers, stemmed, seeded and cut into thin rings*

1 red bell pepper, finely julienned

1 yellow bell pepper, finely julienned

1 green bell pepper, finely julienned

2 carrots, julienned (cut into thin strips)

1 small chocho (chayote), cut into thin strips (optional)

1 large onion, sliced into thin rings

1 cup white or cider vinegar

3 tablespoons tomato paste (or ketchup)

½ cup water

12 whole pimento seeds (allspice berries) (or 1 teaspoon ground allspice)

1 teaspoon sugar

Pinch of salt

METHOD FOR FISH

1. Rinse the fish with water and sprinkle generously with lime juice. Let sit for 20 minutes.
2. Pat fish dry and sprinkle each piece generously with salt, garlic powder and black pepper.
3. Pour the flour into a shallow bowl and dust each fish or filet lightly, shaking off excess. Set aside.
4. Heat about ½-inch of oil in a frying pan until hot (but not smoking) and fry fish until light golden brown and crispy (about 2 minutes per side).
5. Remove fish and drain on paper towels, then arrange in a single layer in glass or casserole dish (or on plates if you don't plan to marinate the fish).
6. Discard the oil.

(continued)

ESCOVEITCH OF RED SNAPPER FILET

(continued)

METHOD FOR SAUCE

1. In a non-reactive saucepan over medium heat, place a tablespoon of oil in the pan.
2. Add the onions, sweet and hot peppers, carrots and chocho and sauté for 2 minutes.
3. Add the vinegar, water, pimento, tomato paste, butter, sugar and salt, and simmer for about 10 minutes or until the vegetables have softened.
4. You can remove the Scotch bonnet slices at this point or leave them in, whichever you prefer.
5. Remove from heat and cool to lukewarm, about 20 minutes, then pour the marinade over the fish. (Make sure it's not too hot or you will overcook the fish.)
6. You can serve the dish immediately or allow it to marinate for a few hours to absorb the flavours, but serve it at or near room temperature.
7. To serve, spoon the vegetables and sauce over the snapper and accompany it with Bammy, Hardo Bread or Festival.

SERVES 6.

SELWYN'S TIP
Be very careful!
Do not rub your eyes after handling the
Scotch bonnet peppers and
wash your hands well afterward

CALLALOO AND CODFISH

INGREDIENTS

½ pound saltfish (dried, salted codfish)

½ pound shredded callaloo or Grace canned

1 medium onion (diced)

½ teaspoon black pepper

3 tablespoons of butter

½ a hot chili pepper (ideally Scotch bonnet)

1 red bell pepper (diced)

1 chopped tomato

1 sprig fresh thyme or 1 teaspoon dried thyme

2 tablespoons unsalted butter or margarine

METHOD

1. Cover the saltfish in cold water.
2. Let soak overnight (minimum 4 hours) changing the water several times (this removes most of the salt).
3. Bring a pan of cold water to boil and gently simmer the fish for 20 minutes (until the fish is tender).
4. Remove the fish from water and allow to cool.
5. Remove all bones and skin then flake the flesh of the fish.
6. Melt the butter in a frying pan and add the onion, red bell pepper, chili and thyme.
7. Sauté for about five minutes.
8. Add the callaloo, tomato, flaked fish, butter and ¼ cup of water.
9. Cover and steam for 10 minutes.

Serve with green banana and fried dumplings.

SERVES 6

Holidays with a Caribbean Flavour

BERMUDAN CODFISH CAKES

Bermudans traditionally serve codfish cakes on Good Friday, but they are also eaten year-round. They can be eaten alone or dressed up with a curry-flavoured sauce or other sauce of your choice.

INGREDIENTS

1 pound codfish filets

1 medium Bermuda red onion, chopped

3 garlic cloves, crushed

2 medium Yukon gold potatoes, quartered

2 large eggs

2 teaspoons hot pepper sauce

¼ cup fresh chopped parsley

4 teaspoons fresh chopped thyme

½ teaspoon freshly ground black pepper

¼ cup all-purpose flour

2 cups Panko bread crumbs

¼ cup vegetable oil

2 tablespoons butter

METHOD

1. Prepare the salted cod by rinsing off the excess salt, put into a pan and cover with cold water.

2. Bring to a boil then drain; repeat 2 to 3 times until the water is no longer salty.

3. Meanwhile, cook the potatoes in a separate pot until soft, about 15 minutes. Drain the fish in a colander and flake the filets. Drain the potatoes in a separate colander. Place the potatoes back in their pot and mash them.

4. In a frying pan over medium heat, add butter. When melted, add onions, garlic, codfish, thyme and sauté for two minutes.

5. Mix the codfish mixture and potatoes in a large bowl. Don't over mix—make sure chunks of cod are visible.

6. In a separate bowl, combine eggs, hot sauce, parsley, salt, and pepper to taste, stirring well to blend.

7. Add the flour and blend well. Gently fold the egg mixture into the codfish mixture. In ½ cup servings, form the mixture into six codfish cakes or patties about ½-inch thick. Spread the bread crumbs on a tray and coat each codfish cake.

8. In a large skillet, heat the oil over medium heat. Fry the codfish cakes for approximately 8 minutes per side, or until golden.

HOT SAUCE OPTIONS

Homemade pepper sauce.

Grace has a variety of hot sauces.

Throughout the Caribbean; English, Spanish or French speaking, the Islands are steeped in traditions. None more so than at Easter time which tends to be a solemn occasion. It all starts with Ash Wednesday, and depending on your religious beliefs, that's when you give up meat.

Easter Traditions in the Caribbean

Easter eggs in Jamaica, Barbados and other islands play an important role. Tradition holds that an egg white placed in a glass container of water on Holy Thursday will form a pattern by Good Friday that can be used to predict the future. Many popular patterns include ships indicating that the person will be traveling, usually to their delight. But no one wants to see a pattern of a coffin for obvious reasons.

Kite flying is another popular pastime on many islands like Bermuda, Trinidad, St. Kitts & Nevis and Grenada. It is said to explain Christ's ascension to heaven.

In rural Jamaica it is believed that cutting the Physic Nut Tree on Good Friday will yield reddish fluid, symbolizing the suffering of Christ.

What would Easter be if we didn't talk about food? Caribbean Easter Dinners are likely to include fish, Easter bun and cheddar cheese. Jamaica is big on Escoveitch fish, Bermuda loves codfish cakes and in the Dominican Republic, traditionally, Mofongo with seafood is popular.

For your next Easter visit to the Caribbean Islands, take the time to observe the traditions, you may be very surprised what you learn.

JAMAICAN EASTER BUN

There's no Easter in Jamaica without the Easter Bun. Whether it's store bought or homemade, this is the supreme Easter food item. It's usually eaten with cheese and some zealous folks enjoy it at breakfast, lunch and dinner—especially on Good Friday when there's no cooking.

INGREDIENTS

- ¼ cup butter
- 1 cup granulated sugar
- 1 bottle Dragon Stout
- ¼ cup orange marmalade
- ¼ cup honey (optional)
- 2 eggs
- 3 cups flour
- 2 teaspoons baking powder
- 1 teaspoon nutmeg
- 1 teaspoon cinnamon
- 1 teaspoon allspice
- 1 tablespoon brown colouring
- 1 cup mixed fruits (raisins, cherries, mixed peel)
- 3 teaspoons vanilla extract

METHOD

1. Melt butter, sugar and stout together.
2. Add marmalade and honey.
3. Mix well and allow to cool.
4. Add slightly beaten eggs, brown colouring (optional) and vanilla.
5. Add mixed fruits, mix well.
6. Sift flour, baking powder (all dry ingredients) together.
7. Add dry mixture to liquid mixture.
8. Pour well mixed batter into greased loaf pan.
9. Bake at 325°F for 15 minutes.
10. Reduce heat to 300°F.
11. Continue baking for approximately 1 hour.
12. Remove from oven and allow to cool.
13. Serve sliced with cheese.

SERVES 8

MOFONGO WITH SPICY SHRIMP

Mofongo is garlic-flavored mashed plantains and is popular in the Dominican Republic, and is also one of the primary dishes found in Puerto Rico .

INGREDIENTS FOR THE MOFONGO

- 2 cups vegetable oil for frying
- 6 unripe plantains
- 4 cloves of garlic, mashed

INGREDIENTS FOR SPICY SHRIMP SAUCE

- 1½ pounds jumbo shrimp peel and deveined
- 1 medium onions, diced
- 2 cloves of garlic, mashed
- 1 medium tomato, diced
- 2 teaspoons tomato paste
- 2 red chili peppers, chopped
- 1 sprig cilantro, chopped
- 1 sprig coriander, chopped
- ½ cup white wine
- Salt and pepper to taste

METHOD FOR MOFONGO

1. In a sauce pan heat a tablespoon of oil over very low heat and cook the garlic for 1 min add 2 teaspoon of salt. Remove from heat and reserve.
2. In a deep frying pan heat the remaining oil and fry the plantains until golden brown all over.
3. Using a pilon (wooden mortar) mash the plantains and garlic together, leaving the middle hollow.
4. Fill with some of the sautéed shrimp, turn mortar upside down onto plate and garnish with a bit more shrimp and sauce

METHOD FOR SPICY SHRIMP SAUCE

1. In frying pan, heat 2 tablespoons of oil, add onion and garlic, sauté for 2 minutes
2. Add shrimp and sauté for another 2 minutes.
3. Add tomato paste, white wine, diced tomato, chili peppers, salt and pepper to taste.
4. Add 2 tablespoons of butter and finish with chopped coriander and cilantro.

Beef and pork are favourite accompaniments to mofongo

Holiday Ham
Varieties and Terminology

The term ham is usually restricted to a cut of pork. Ham can either be dry cured or wet cured. A dry cured ham has been rubbed in a mixture containing salt and a variety of other ingredients, including sugar, followed by a period of drying and aging. Wet cured ham is cured with a brine followed by dry aging or smoking. It can also be cooked and served fresh which is the recipe we're using here, for those of you adventurous souls who like a little challenge. This recipe is simple yet fresh and full of flavour.

A lot of people stay away from pork products because of religious prohibitions. Jewish, Muslim, Seventh-day Adventist and Rastafarian faiths dietary laws do not permit the consumption of ham. But during the festive seasons of Thanksgiving, Christmas and Easter, the ham is king and a must have for those who crave that other white meat (not chicken).

There are a variety of names given to this cut of meat
- **Prosciutto** which is a must have for all Italians
- **Virginia Ham** for the American taste
- **Black Forest** for Germans
- **Yorkshire** for the Englishman
- ...and of course **The West Indian,** who are big on Jerk.

Processed turkey, ham or chicken products are always available. Whatever is on your table for the holiday season, remember to serve it with a lot of love.

HONEY CINNAMON GLAZED HAM
WITH PINEAPPLE RELISH AND MIXED BERRIES

INGREDIENTS FOR HAM

    1 leg or shoulder of fresh pork 10 to 15 pounds

    Water for blanching

    6 bay leaves

    12 pimento berries

    2 tablespoons cloves

    4 tablespoons salt

    2 tablespoons black pepper

    2 cups brown sugar

    2 tablespoons malt vinegar

    2 tablespoons dry thyme

METHOD FOR HAM

1. Wrap meat in Saran Wrap (this prevents meat from tearing) and place in large stock pot.
2. Fill pot three quarters full with cold water.
3. Add all the seasonings and cover with lid or foil paper.
4. Blanch for one and a half hours.
5. Remove from water and let cool. This can be done overnight and refrigerated.
6. Core meat diagonally in 1-inch squares and place cloves in grooves.
7. Place on rack in baking pan and bake in oven at 350ºF for three and a half hours or until juices run clear.
8. Baste every half an hour with the honey cinnamon glaze (see next page for recipe).

INGREDIENTS FOR HONEY CINNAMON GLAZE

    1 cup honey

    3 cups orange juice

    2 cups brown sugar

    1 cup butter

    1 tablespoon ground cinnamon

    1 tablespoon allspice

    1 tablespoon ground nutmeg

METHOD FOR HONEY CINNAMON GLAZE

1. In a sauce pan, melt butter, add sugar and honey.
2. Bring to a boil and add all the other ingredients, stirring constantly for 5 minutes so as not to overflow.
3. If you are using smoked ham there is no need to blanch, just core the ham, place on rack in baking pan and roast in oven at 350ºF for one and a half hours, basting every half hour.

continued on next page

PINEAPPLE RELISH WITH FRESH BERRIES

This recipe is a fusion of fresh berries, typically found in North America, with the pineapple and hot pepper sauce for a Caribbean kick. Use as an accompaniment to Honey Cinnamon Glazed Ham recipe on previous page.

INGREDIENTS

- 1 can pineapple, chopped
- 1 pint raspberry
- 1 pint blackberry
- ½ pint strawberry (cut in quarters)
- 2 cups pineapple juice
- 2 cups brown sugar
- 1 cup butter
- 1 tablespoon hot pepper sauce (optional)

METHOD

1. In a sauce pan, melt butter, add sugar and pineapple juice.
2. Bring to a boil and add pineapple, berries and simmer for 10 minutes.
3. Add chopped parsley for colour.

On "Turkey Day" why not try something new? Maybe, create a combination of your own recipe with an original idea that your dinner guests are sure to be pleased with. You may even have more room in that oven for all the other trimmings this time.

There's More Than One Way to Prepare a Thanksgiving Turkey

If you're looking for something a little different this year, here are my choices for creating a turkey wonder that's a bit different from the norm—and just as tasty to eat.

GRILLED TURKEY. We put everything else on the grill. Why not the turkey? Grilling a turkey gives it a unique flavour and texture much like chicken parts grilled to perfection for a family outing. The difference is that here we are grilling an entire turkey at once. Instead of putting the turkey on the grill slats, it is placed in a baking pan over the flames. This way, the turkey can be basted and seasoned prior to and during the cooking process. As the turkey nears doneness, add your favourite sauce to it for an extra kick.

FRIED TURKEY. Who would have thought you could ever fry a turkey? I don't know who thought of it, but let me tell you I'm glad they did. A deep fried turkey is delicious.

Many people think there is not a pan big enough to fry an entire turkey and up until several years ago, they were right. Not that long ago we started to see turkey fryers everywhere. Pour peanut oil (or your favourite cooking oil) in a large frying pot, once the oil reaches a certain temperature, a clean and dry turkey is slowly lowered into it. The turkey can be seasoned beforehand or injected with a marinade to seal in flavour. It takes at least an hour to cook a turkey thoroughly. Depending on your marinade on the outside, the skin will be crispy and dark, but don't worry. That crunchy and tasty skin hides the most tender, perfectly cooked meat beneath.

TURDUCKEN. What is a turducken? Actually it is a combination of various de-boned fowl: turkey, duck, and chicken. They are all put together and layered with stuffing to create this newest addition to the Thanksgiving table. The turducken looks like a turkey on the outside, but all you have to do is cut into it to see that it is anything but. Those who have tried it, say that the turducken taste great.

SMOKED TURKEY. If you want a turkey fresh off the coals, try a smoker to cook your turkey this year. The bird is cleaned and seasoned. It can then be injected with a marinade if the cook so chooses. Once the coals have burned hot and come to a temperature, not so hot to burn the outside skin, place the turkey on the smoker. It will take several hours for this turkey to cook, but placing a pan of water on the smoker will help hold in moisture and create a juicy yet well smoked turkey for everyone to enjoy.

PLAIN AND SIMPLE ROAST TURKEY

Any type of stuffing works with this roasted turkey. You don't even have to use stuffing if you prefer not to. It tastes great with or without.

INGREDIENTS

1 whole turkey (18 pounds)
5 cups of your favourite stuffing
½ cup unsalted butter, softened
Salt to taste
Pepper to taste
1½ quarts turkey stock

METHOD

1. Clean the turkey by removing the neck and giblets and rinsing the turkey with cold water.
2. Pat the turkey dry with paper towel inside and outside.
3. Bring the oven temperature up to 325°F.
4. Move the rack to the lowest position you can in your oven.
5. Place a roasting rack into a large roasting pan.
6. Stuff the turkey cavity with your favourite stuffing mixture.
7. Rub the turkey skin with the soft butter making sure to cover the whole outside of the turkey.
8. Sprinkle on the salt and pepper to taste.
9. Pour 2 cups of the turkey stock into the bottom of the roasting pan.
10. Place the turkey breast side up on the rack in the pan.
11. Make a tent out of aluminum foil to completely cover the turkey but not cover the roasting pan.
12. Place the turkey in the oven and allow roasting for 2½ hours. Baste the turkey every 30 minutes with the stock in the roasting pan.
13. If the stock should evaporate, add 2 cups to the roasting pan and continue adding as necessary 1 to 2 cups at a time.
14. After 2½ hours, remove the aluminum foil and continue roasting for another 1½ hours or until a meat thermometer reaches 180°F when inserted into the thigh.
15. Be sure to continue basting every 30 minutes during the last 1½ hours of roasting.

SERVES 12.

SELWYN'S TIP

Remove turkey from the oven and place on a large platter for at least 30 minutes before carving

Thinking of pumpkin as a nutritious super food can be a bit puzzling. After all, isn't the image that comes to mind sweet and smooth and covered in whipped cream? But, according to nutritionists, we should be thinking of pumpkin more often than during Halloween, the annual Charlie Brown cartoon or as a delicious way to top off a scrumptious Thanksgiving dinner.

The Pumpkin Puzzle
A Super Food
Getting Its Just Desserts

Pumpkin is a vegetable, regardless of those images. In fact, pumpkin is a nutrient-rich super food that has a great number of health benefits. Let's take a look at why pumpkin should get its just desserts... beyond desserts.

A WELL-ROUNDED VEGETABLE

The list of nutrients in pumpkin is almost endless. Starting with the basic vitamins and minerals we all know, pumpkin has a healthy amount of vitamins C and E, and is a rich source of potassium and magnesium. Pumpkin is also right up there with other super foods in the dietary fiber category.

Pumpkin also contains two lesser known elements called carotenoids, which are alpha-carotene and beta-carotene. These carotenoids are fat-soluble compounds that are specifically linked to decreasing the risk of a number of cancers, as well as lowering the risk for heart disease, cataracts, and macular degeneration.

Beta carotene is an important antioxidant. Foods rich in beta carotene, like pumpkin, sweet potatoes, and carrots, have the potential to lower cholesterol and to slow the aging process of our vital organs. Antioxidant rich foods, like pumpkin, are key to fighting the free radicals which attack our healthy cells.

And it's not just the flesh, the inside of the pumpkin is also healthy. The seeds from the pumpkin also earn super food status. These seeds, or pepitas, are also nutrient-rich and beneficial, containing high concentrations of magnesium, phosphorous, zinc, copper, selenium, and other nutrients. The seeds also have essential Omega 3 fatty acids and even the amino acid tryptophan, known for its anti-depressant benefits. So, as you see, the pumpkin has a lot more to offer than you might think.

THINKING OUTSIDE THE PIE PAN

Of course, pumpkin is associated first with pie. Beyond pie, many folks know about making pumpkin muffins or cake. These are great and delicious, but trying to branch out into more pumpkin dishes takes a little more imagination.

But, first to clarify; no, pumpkin does not taste like pumpkin pie. That flavour comes from the spices used in the pie, like nutmeg, allspice, and cinnamon. Because pumpkin basically has very little flavour of its own, it will taste like whatever you want it to taste like.

NUTMEG   ALLSPICE   CINNAMON

Pumpkin is truly versatile enough to go into soup, chowder, stews, casseroles, and other main dishes. You can puree pumpkin and add to soups as a thickener and to add great fiber and nutrition. Try roasting pumpkin and mashing like you would any squash. Flavour with herbs, salt, and pepper for added taste. You can steam it, boil it, or puree it to use in a variety of other recipes, like pumpkin pancakes for breakfast. The seeds, of course, can be roasted in a number of ways, then added to cereal, trail mix, or salads.

For a real different twist, and a very pretty presentation, scoop out the flesh from several small pumpkins, chop up and add to your choice of meat, vegetables, rice or bread cubes, and seasonings. Then stuff the pumpkin shells with the mixture and bake to make an entrée that your guests won't soon forget.

The pumpkin has definitely earned its place among the top super foods for a healthy diet. Colourful, nutritious, delicious, and oh so versatile—all the things a super food should be!

Turkey has been a mainstay on the Christmas Day table for centuries. Turkey has gained quite the measure of importance in many societies but honestly, Tom the Turkey doesn't always want to be the center of attention—especially at dinner.

Alternatives to the Turkey

Many people are substituting other dishes as the main dish for the Christmas meal. Maybe you are not having a big family get-together this year and everyone is fending for themselves. If that is the case, there is no need to fix a fifteen pound turkey with all the trimmings and dessert for less than a handful of people.

Increasingly, more people are jumping on the vegetarian bandwagon. For these folks, meat will not be on the menu for Christmas dinner. This is not what the majority of people consider a traditional holiday, but Christmas doesn't stop because there is no meat on the table. Traditions are created differently for everyone's lifestyles and beliefs and vegetarians can celebrate the same holiday everyone else does, just minus the turkey.

Health is also a big concern for many of us. More and more people are cutting back on what they eat in exchange for a healthier, longer life. Christmas is one of, if not the biggest eating holiday of the year. In decreasing the amounts and types of food they eat, these health conscious people are making other choices for the meal to reflect their improved wellbeing.

One alternative to turkey is fish. Many fish, like salmon, are high in omega-3 fatty acids -- good for lowering cholesterol in the body. A main dish of salmon with wild rice and green beans satisfies the palate and does wonders for the body as well. To jazz up that salmon, add a pecan or parmesan crust.

What about chicken? A roasted chicken is smaller than a turkey for a more intimate gathering. A small whole chicken can be barbecued or fried, or both, depending on your taste buds. There is less cooking time as well which is always a plus if you ask the chef. You can even prepare the chicken earlier in the day and then warm it up for the full-fledged dinner.

For some, Christmas just would not be the same without turkey. For one reason or another they don't need or want a big 20 pound turkey. Instead, choose a roasted turkey breast or turkey cutlets. They bake up quickly and leave less of a mess to clean up after dinner.

There doesn't have to be meat on the table at all as vegetarians will tell you. Set the table with a variety of casserole dishes. Rice and broccoli casserole, macaroni and cheese, green bean casserole, and other vegetable dishes can fill you up and keep you from missing the turkey. Some vegetarians create a tofu turkey as their centerpiece as well to help set the "mood" for the occasion.

The menu for Christmas is not set in stone. The meal allows us to gather in celebration and to share that good feeling, no matter what food items are or aren't on the table.

THE PERFECT TURKEY

INGREDIENTS

1 (18 pound) whole turkey, neck and giblets, removed

2 cups kosher salt

½ cup butter, melted

2 large onions, peeled and chopped

4 carrots, peeled and chopped

4 stalks celery, chopped

2 sprigs fresh thyme

1 bay leaf

1 cup dry white wine

METHOD

1. Rub the turkey inside and out with kosher salt.
2. Place the bird in a large stock pot, and cover with cold water.
3. Place in the refrigerator, and allow the turkey to soak in the salt and water mixture 12 hours, or overnight.
4. Preheat oven to 350°F.
5. Thoroughly rinse the turkey, and discard the brine mixture.
6. Brush the turkey with ½ the melted butter.
7. Place breast side up on a roasting rack in a shallow roasting pan.
8. Stuff the turkey cavity with 1 onion, ½ the carrots, ½ the celery, 1 sprig of thyme and the bay leaf.
9. Scatter the remaining vegetables and thyme around the bottom of the roasting pan, and cover with the white wine.
10. Roast uncovered 3½ to 4 hours in the preheated oven, until the internal temperature of the thigh reaches 180°F.
11. About ⅔ through the roasting time, brush with the remaining butter.
12. Allow the bird to stand about 30 minutes before carving.

SERVES 12-16

BERMUDAN CASSAVA PIE

This recipe is from my good friend Arnold Minors. Cassava pie is always a Bermudan favourite! It is traditionally served at Christmas, Easter and sporting events. I was told Bermuda is the only Caribbean Island that makes it and recipes are passed down from generation to generation. The cassava pie is often taken overseas to be shared with friends and relatives during the festive season.

INGREDIENTS

- 3½ pounds chicken
- 6 pounds cassava, grated
- 1 can condensed milk
- 1 pound butter, melted
- 1½ tablespoon salt
- 2 teaspoons nutmeg
- 2 teaspoons cinnamon
- 1 teaspoon cloves
- 12 eggs
- 1 pound sugar
- 1 tablespoon vanilla
- Black rum, to taste

METHOD

1. Divide the dough in two portions and place half the mixture in the base of a large, well-greased, baking pan (you need about a 3cm depth of batter on the bottom).
2. Meanwhile, put the chicken in a large pot. Cover with water, season to taste, then bring to a boil.
3. Reduce to a simmer and cook until the meat is just tender (about 35 minutes).
4. Turn off the heat and remove the chicken from the pan. When it's cool enough to be handled, remove the chicken meat from the bones and ladle the meat over the cassava batter, adding a little stock (reserve the remaining stock).
5. Cover the meat filling with the remaining batter and form a little hole in the centre of the dough so that steam can escape. (Make indentations in rows with the back of a fork).
6. Place in a pre-heated oven to 350°F and bake for about 60 minutes then reduce the oven temperature to 200°F.
7. Bake for a further 3 hours. Baste every hour by pouring a little of the stock through the hole in the top of pie.
8. Allow to cool in the pan.

To serve, cut into slices; warm in the oven or fry in butter.

STRAWBERRY JAMMED CHRISTMAS COOKIES

These cookies make a pretty addition to any buffet. They are easy to prepare and fun to eat. Any type of seedless jam works great in this recipe.

INGREDIENTS

1 cup of butter, room temperature

1 (3 ounce) package cream cheese, room temperature

1 cup of sugar

1 egg yolk

3 teaspoons of vanilla extract

2½ cups of flour

seedless strawberry jam

METHOD

1. Place the butter, cream cheese and sugar in a bowl.
2. Cream the mixture with an electric mixer until light and fluffy.
3. Add the egg yolk and vanilla and beat until blended in well.
4. Stir in the flour until well combined.
5. Cover the bowl and chill for at least 1 hour to firm up the dough.
6. Pre-set the oven temperature to 350°F.
7. Remove the dough and shape into 1-inch balls. Place the balls 2-inches apart on an ungreased cookie sheet.
8. Use the handle of a wooden spoon to make ½-inch indentations in the center of each cookie ball.
9. Fill each indentation with strawberry jam.
10. Bake 10 minutes or until the cookies are set.
11. Cool on the cookie sheet 2 minutes then move to wire racks to finish cooling.

MAKES 5 DOZEN COOKIES.

Desserts or Bake-Bake

BANANA BREAD

Banana is now the global fruit and is easily accessible. Try this easy recipe for a satisfying ending to your dinner or as a snack.

INGREDIENTS

3 or 4 very ripe bananas, smashed

⅓ cup melted butter

1 cup sugar (can easily reduce to ¾ cup)

1 egg, beaten

1 teaspoon vanilla

1 teaspoon baking soda

Pinch of salt

1½ cups of all-purpose flour

METHOD

1. Preheat the oven to 350ºF.
2. Mix butter into the mashed bananas in a large mixing bowl.
3. Mix in the sugar, egg, and vanilla.
4. Sprinkle the baking soda and salt over the mixture and mix in.
5. Add the flour last, mix all ingredients together.
6. Pour mixture into a buttered 4x8-inch loaf pan.
7. Bake for 1 hour.
8. Cool on a rack.
9. Remove from pan and slice to serve.

SERVES 6 - 8

SELWYN'S TIP

You can make this banana recipe your own by adding any of these options: Cup of raisins, a teaspoon of cinnamon, or a cup of your favourite chopped nuts. Elevate this comfort food by arranging caramelized bananas on the side or even top with a cream cheese frosting

CARROT MUFFINS

INGREDIENTS

1 cup raisins

2 cups warm water

2 cups all-purpose flour

1 tablespoon baking powder

2 teaspoons baking soda

1 teaspoon salt

1 teaspoon ground cinnamon

4 eggs

1 cup vegetable oil

¾ cup brown sugar

3 cups shredded carrots

METHOD

1. Combine raisins and water in a small bowl.
2. Let soak for 15 minutes.
3. Drain raisins, discard water and set raisins aside.
4. Preheat oven to 350°F.
5. Grease muffin cups or line with paper muffin liners.
6. In a large bowl, sift together flour, baking powder, baking soda, salt and cinnamon.
7. In a separate bowl, combine eggs, oil and brown sugar; beat well.
8. Combine egg mixture and flour mixture; mix just until moistened.
9. Fold in carrots and drained raisins.
10. Spoon into prepared muffin cups.
11. Bake in preheated oven for 20 to 30 minutes.
12. Let cool for 30 minutes before frosting.

MAKES 8 - 12

A LITTLE DIFFERENT APPLE PIE-A-LA MODE

Many diasporan dinner tables seamlessly integrate the foods of North America with foods from their native isles. It's not unusual to find Codfish Cakes for appetizers, Rice and Peas with Jerk Chicken for the main meal, a Garden Tomato Basil salad and a pie-a-la mode for dessert. See sample menus for more. Here's a little different apple pie recipe.

INGREDIENTS

$1\frac{1}{3}$ cups + 2 tablespoons of flour, divided

8 tablespoons + 2 teaspoons of sugar, divided

¼ teaspoon of salt

½ cup of cold butter, broken up

4 tablespoons + 1 teaspoon of cold water

¼ teaspoon of vanilla extract

3 cups of tart apples, peeled and chopped

6 tablespoons of sugar

½ teaspoon cinnamon

4 tablespoons caramel ice cream topping, warm

METHOD

1. Toss together $1\frac{1}{3}$ cups of flour, 2 tablespoons of sugar and the salt in a mixing bowl.
2. Cut the butter into the mixture with a pastry blender until crumbly.
3. Gradually add the cold water and vanilla while tossing with a fork.
4. Continue tossing after all the water and vanilla has been added until a soft dough forms.
5. Form the dough into a ball, cover with plastic wrap and chill for 30 minutes.
6. Set the oven temperature to 400ºF and allow it to preheat.
7. Line a baking sheet with parchment paper.
8. Lightly flour a flat surface and roll the chilled ball of dough into a circle.
9. Place the dough on the prepared baking sheet.
10. Place the apples, 6 tablespoon of sugar and remaining flour into a mixing bowl.
11. Stir until the apples are completely covered with the flour and sugar.
12. Spread the apple mixture into the middle of the dough leaving a 2-inch wide edge.
13. Fold the edges of dough up over the filling leaving the center uncovered.
14. Toss the remaining sugar and cinnamon together and sprinkle over the open filling.
15. Bake 25 minutes or until the filling is bubbly and crust is golden brown.
16. Slide the pie onto a wire rack to cool.
17. Drizzle with the caramel topping before serving.

MAKES 12 SERVINGS

MANGO CHEESECAKE

INGREDIENTS FOR THE CRUST

    1½ cups graham cracker crumbs

    ½ cup sugar

    6 tablespoons (¾ stick) unsalted butter, melted

INGREDIENTS FOR THE FILLING

    3 large very ripe mangoes (each about 13 ounces), peeled, pitted, coarsely chopped

    3 (8-oz) packages cream cheese, room temperature

    1¼ cups sugar

    2 teaspoons vanilla extract

    4 large eggs

    Sliced, peeled, pitted mangoes

METHOD FOR THE CRUST

1. Preheat oven to 325°F.
2. Lightly butter 9-inch-diameter spring form pan with 2¾-inch high sides.
3. Stir cracker crumbs and sugar in medium bowl to blend.
4. Add melted butter and stir until evenly moistened.
5. Press crumb mixture firmly onto bottom (not sides) of prepared pan.
6. Bake until crust is set, about 12 minutes.
7. Cool completely.
8. Maintain oven temperature.

METHOD FOR FILLING AND CAKE

1. Puree mangoes in processor until smooth.
2. Set aside 2 cups mango puree (reserve any remaining puree for another use).
3. Beat cream cheese, sugar, and vanilla in large bowl until smooth.
4. Add eggs 1 at a time, beating well after each addition.
5. Add 2 cups mango puree and beat until well blended.
6. Pour filling over crust in pan.
7. Bake cake until set and puffed and golden around edges (center may move very slightly when pan is gently shaken), about 1 hour 25 minutes.
8. Cool cake 1 hour.
9. Refrigerate uncovered overnight.
10. Run small knife between cake and sides of pan to loosen.
11. Remove pan sides.
12. Transfer cake to platter.
13. Cut into wedges and serve with sliced mangoes.

We try to save money on our food bills. Fresh fruits and veggies seem to cost more and spoil quicker. If you love to eat fresh fruits, here is one way to be sure they won't spoil.

Make That Fruit Last Longer.
Dry It

Dried fruits can serve as a healthy alternative to candy. Instead of reaching for chocolate or a piece of hard candy, the kids will reach for dried pineapple or apple slices. The sweetness of the fruit is concentrated when it is dried and bursts forth with every bite.

Learning to dry fruit is a fairly easy process. You don't need to buy any fancy equipment. Investing in a few sealing jars would be nice so that storing the fruit will be easier. Sealing jars can be found fairly inexpensive at many supermarkets. Gather fruits you want to dry. Some of the more common ones are: pineapples, apples, plums, grapes, apricots, and tomatoes (yes, they're a fruit!). If you favour lemons, limes and other citrus fruits, you will be drying the peels and not the fruit itself.

All fruit and equipment need to be clean and thoroughly dried before beginning. Drying racks are needed if you plan on air drying outside or using an oven. Some pieces may be done before others so rotating the trays in the oven gives you a chance to remove any fruit that is already dried and replace with another.

Slice the fruit into small pieces. Apples need to be cored and peeled before slicing. Tomatoes can be cut into slices or quarters and salted before drying. Grapes and plums are okay as is because the skin doesn't affect their taste. If you prefer to use the microwave to dry your fruit, place small batches in the microwave on the turntable tray. Fruit pieces should be evenly spaced to allow for air circulation while drying. Set the microwave to the defrost setting in order to dry the fruit. It will take about thirty to forty-five minutes. Check after thirty minutes and gradually add time as needed. It is not recommended that tomatoes be dried via the microwave because they should be dried in the oven at approximately 120°F for about twenty-four hours.

You can eat some of these tasty treats as soon as they are dried or you can save some for later. If storing for later, let the fruit cool before placing in sealing jars or plastic bags. Dried fruits will keep for up to two weeks in a cool dark place. However, these fruit treats are so scrumptious they may not even last for that long.

Dried fruit has a multitude of uses. It can be eaten as is or as a flavourful addition to ice cream, salads, pizzas and more. Drying your fruits will save you money because it makes the fruit last longer than normal, avoid spoilage and gives you a reason to eat more of it.

STRAWBERRY SURPRISE FREEZER JAM

1 pint boxes of fresh strawberries, washed, drained and hulls removed

2½ cups of fresh pineapple, peeled and finely chopped

7 cups sugar

2 packages (1¾ ounce) powdered pectin

1 cup cold water

4 pint freezer containers with lids

METHOD

1. Place strawberries in a large mixing bowl.
2. Crush the strawberries with a potato masher.
3. Measure out 2½ cups strawberries and place in a separate bowl.
4. Add the pineapple to the strawberries.
5. Slowly add the sugar and stir until well combined.
6. Place the cold water in a saucepan over medium heat.
7. Add the pectin.
8. Stir continuously until water begins to boil.
9. Boil 1 minute.
10. Remove from heat.
11. Pour the water mixture into the fruit.
12. Stir well to combine.
13. Continue stirring 4 minutes.
14. Pour into the pint freezer containers and cover.
15. Let stand at room temperature for 24 hours.
16. Freeze after 24 hours.
17. Jam will stay good in the freezer for up to 6 months.
18. To use, remove from freezer and allow to come to room temperature, about 1 hour.
19. Cover and refrigerate for up to 3 weeks.

SERVES 6

Do you picture snacks helping your heart and lowering your cholesterol while filling you up between meals?

Snacking has gotten a bad name through the years, mostly due to the over-abundance of pre-packaged snack foods. But, snacking doesn't have to be bad for you if you know what snacks to choose. As a matter of fact, snacking can be really good for you. Let's take a look at one healthy food that should be considered an essential snack.

The Nutty News.
A Super Food Headliner
in a Tiny Package

Nutrition by the Handful

That little nut you have been snacking on is really a super food because of the unique combination of fats, protein, vitamins and minerals. This tiny powerhouse works hard lowering the risk of some significant diseases and health conditions.

Don't let the fat content or calorie count of nuts worry you too much. Even though nuts are often high in calories and fat, they have 'good' fats and omega 3 fatty acids that lower bad cholesterol levels and help regulate blood pressure and healthy heart rhythms. The fiber content in nuts also helps control cholesterol and has been found to lower the risk for diabetes.

But that's not all. Certain types of nuts also have plant sterols which is another cholesterol inhibitor. It is so important as a cholesterol inhibitor, as a matter of fact, that plant sterols are added to things like orange juice and margarine for the health benefits. And you've got it all right there in a nut.

In addition, vitamin E and the amino acid L-arginine are two elements that help reduce plaque in the circulatory system, which helps to prevent clots in arteries. Nuts have so many of these healthy elements that they may be one of the most powerful food you can eat to take care of your heart.

Enjoy Nuts in Numerous Ways

The important thing to remember with nuts is, like many other things in life, too much of a good thing isn't really good. Since nuts are dense in calories and fat, a little goes a long way. For instance, just a dozen or so cashews can have up to 180 calories. For this reason, health experts recommend limiting your daily intake of most nuts to no more than a couple of ounces. This is actually good news for your budget, since adding nuts to your healthy diet requires only a small investment for such a big return.

So, what specific nuts are best to eat regularly? There isn't really a lot of definitive research to suggest one type of nut is better than another. Walnuts, almonds, peanuts, and cashews are popular and easy to find in most regions. You'll also find many recipes for these particular nuts, so it's easy to incorporate nuts into your meals as well as your snacking.

Consider substituting chopped nuts for the chocolate chips in cookies, for example. Toss peanuts or almonds into a green salad or pasta salad for added nutrition and crunch. Use natural peanut butter on your morning toast instead of butter or jam. Walnuts are a classic choice to top a savoury salad. Chop almonds up and toss in your vanilla yogurt for a nice crunch.

You can also grind almonds, peanuts, or other nuts into a coarse meal. Use this meal to coat chicken or fish instead of using cornmeal or flour when frying or baking. Grind the meal fine and add to smoothies in your blender. Almonds can be ground into a flour consistency and can be used in many dishes as a substitute for wheat flour. This gluten-free flour alternative has become very popular in recent years.

It's best to buy shelled, unsalted, or minimally processed varieties of nuts in small quantities. You can also protect fresh nuts from oxidation by storing them in a cool, dark, dry place. Or you can store nuts in an airtight container in the refrigerator or freezer. The oils that naturally occur in nuts can become rancid if exposed to heat and air.

Adding small amounts of nuts to your diet will provide your body with big benefits. Choose a variety of nuts, store them properly, and enjoy a handful of crunchy nutrition every day.

EASY WALNUT COOKIE SQUARES

INGREDIENTS

1 cup flour

¼ teaspoon salt

¼ teaspoon baking soda

2 cups brown sugar, packed

2 cups walnuts, chopped

2 eggs

1 teaspoon vanilla extract

METHOD

1. Preheat oven to 325°F and line baking sheet with parchment paper.
2. In large bowl, stir together the flour, salt and baking soda.
3. Add the brown sugar and walnuts and mix until blended well.
4. In separate bowl, whisk eggs together with vanilla extract.
5. Stir egg mixture into dry mixture and stir until combined.
6. Press dough onto bottom of baking sheet.
7. Bake in preheated oven at 325°F for 12 to 15 minutes or until browned lightly.
8. Remove and let cool on rack, then cut into squares.

SERVES 4

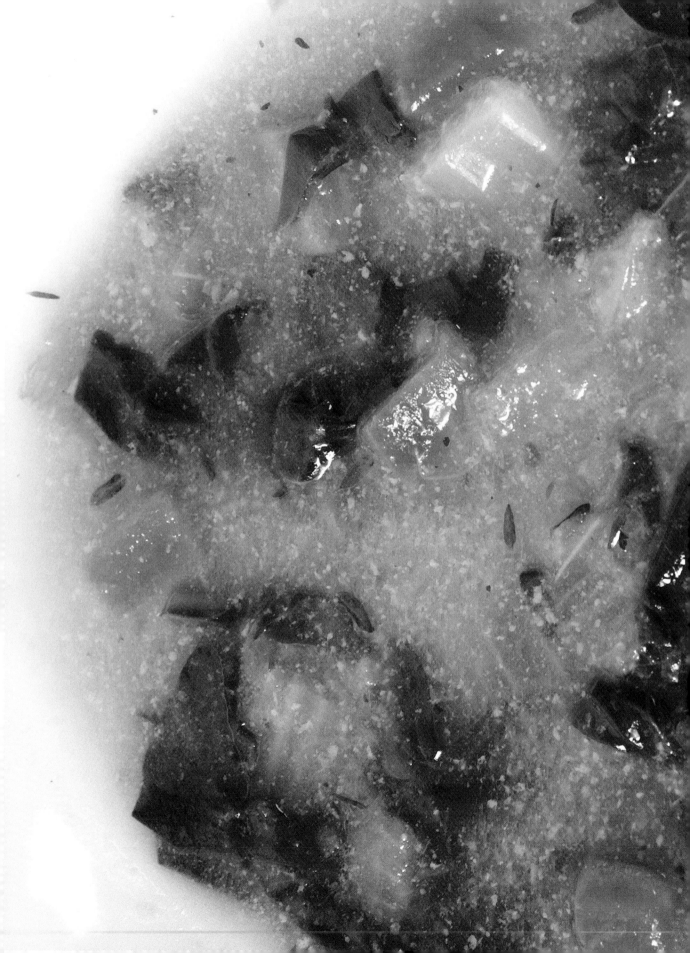

Soup Du Jour

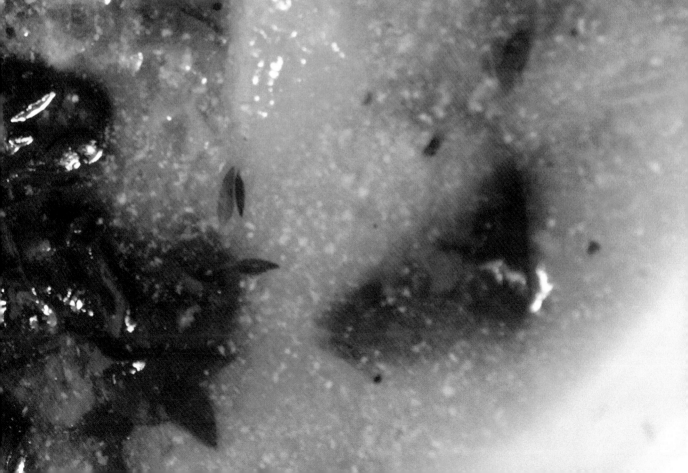

In this day and age it can be a challenge to eat healthy. With your busy schedule, especially if you have children, it's easier to quickly grab whatever is available and deal with the health consequences later. With the following tips for "soups on the go," you'll learn how to make sure that the food you grab is a healthy choice.

Healthy Homemade Soups on the Go

The problem with dealing with the consequences of unhealthy eating habits is that later is actually closer than you might think. Later is right now. Sadly, we are a nation of obese adults and just as many, if not more, obese children. Our unhealthy eating choices have caught up with us. You might be asking yourself, "How can I eat healthy when I'm crunched for time already?"

One way is to make foods that can be taken with you on the go. One of those foods is soup. Soup is tasty, filling, and good for you anytime, but especially on a cold fall or winter day. There are hot soups and believe it or not even cold soups. Many of the warm soups are even good eaten cold or lukewarm.

First, choose your favourite soup. A popular choice of many is the infamous chicken noodle soup. There's nothing better when you are under the weather than the warm chicken broth soothing your throat. Campbell's has a wonderful soup in a microwave container perfect for eating on the go, but we are going to make our own soup for an even healthier choice.

The one thing that is best about homemade food is that you know what is and is not in it. Since we are concerned with health, preparing your own soup creations at home is the best way to go. No matter which type of soup you choose to make, be sure to use fresh ingredients. The other items you'll need are plenty of cups with lids and a blender.

Now it's time to actually create your time-saving soup. A good soup always starts with the stock. For chicken soup, make the broth by boiling the remains of the chicken you had for dinner. Add the herbs and seasonings of your choice and boil until the chicken bones are clean. Any remaining meat will be included in the broth. Once the broth cools completely, ladle it into air-tight jars or containers for storing.

If you're more of a beef and vegetable soup lover, you can use commercial canned broths or bouillon cubes for the base of your soup. Season the stock really well and boil before adding any other ingredients. Once the stock is ready, all that is left to do is toss in your favourite veggies. Again, wait until the soup is completely cooled before pouring into storage or serving containers.

Now, what about that blender? It's a bit difficult to eat soup the traditional way while driving and if you are serving to your kids, the combination of a car and soup in a bowl is a disaster waiting to happen. Here's where the blender comes into the picture.

Pour some of the soup into the blender and blend until the pieces are small enough for you to swallow without choking. You can even puree the soup completely if you'd prefer. For a thicker texture, add a bit of cream soup. Now, your soup is ready for distributing in your to-go cups.

The ideal cup would be a coffee mug with a lid. These types of cups have a wide opening that's perfect for drinking soups. Be sure to prepare enough soup for the entire week. You can take the soup with you while you're out shopping, working in the garden or to work. A cup of soup is packed with healthy nutrients and it won't mess up the car or cramp your busy lifestyle. The next time you don't have time to eat, reach for a cup of healthy homemade soup instead of pulling into that fast food drive-thru.

Here are some quick soup ideas to get you started.

Beef and Vegetable Soup

Brown hamburger meat and onion in a little butter or olive oil. Once the meat is tender, add diced vegetables and tomatoes. I usually add kidney beans (red or white whatever you like). Canned plum tomatoes with fresh herbs will add a lot of flavours. The quantity of each ingredient isn't important. Just throw the meal together and add seasoning to taste and you'll have a hearty soup.

Chicken Noodle Soup

Bring chicken broth to a boil and add a handful of noodles. Add diced vegetables and some cooked chicken. I use either leftover chicken or turkey. Season to taste. You can easily adapt this for chicken and rice soup by using quick cooking rice instead of noodles.

Bean Soup

Heat chicken stock and water and add diced tomatoes and any combination of canned beans to the soup—drain and rinse them first. Season the soup with salt and pepper to taste.

By the way, if you don't have any stock on hand, just use water and add one or two bouillon cubes.

I also like to keep dry lentils and split peas around since both of them cook rather quickly (especially compared to dry beans). With either one of them, I start by sautéing an onion and some garlic in oil, then add water and the dry lentils or peas along with some bouillon cubes and bring it to a boil. If you have ham or bacon in the fridge, throw a bit of that in for flavour as well and let the soup cook until everything is tender.

JAMAICAN PEPPERPOT SOUP OR STEW

Jamaicans refer to pepperpot as a soup made with callaloo (spinach), Grace Coconut Milk and various type of meats e.g. chicken. Pepperpot is Guyana's national dish. It is typically a stew with cassareep - a special sauce made from cassava root, beef, pork, dashine leaves and all kinds of niceties. When you order 'pepperpot' you will indeed get a different dish depending on what island you're on or which restaurant. On this page and the next, I'll give you the recipe for both the soup and stew.

INGREDIENTS

1 bunch fresh callaloo or spinach

1 medium onion

2 large carrots

1 pound yellow yam

1 pound chopped chicken

1 cup Grace Coconut Milk

1 pound pumpkin

4 tablespoons chicken base (or bouillon cubes)

Salt and pepper to taste

3 litres chicken stock or water

2 tablespoons chopped thyme

2 bay leaves

METHOD

1. In a medium stock pot add chicken stock or (water) and bring to a boil.
2. Add raw chicken with thyme, soup base, salt and pepper.
3. Cook for 15 minutes then add diced onions, carrots, yellow yam, pumpkin and Grace Coconut Milk. Cook for another ½ hour.
4. Add callaloo or spinach and simmer for another 15 minutes.

SERVES 8 - 10

GUYANESE STYLE PEPPERPOT WITH CASSAREEP

INGREDIENTS

- 1 pound stewing beef or beef short ribs
- 1 pound pork trotters (or cow foot), optional
- ½ pig tails optional
- ¾ cup cassareep*
- 1 red hot pepper
- 1 cinnamon stick
- 3 tablespoons brown sugar
- 2 tablespoons salt
- 2 tablespoons basil
- 1 bunch chopped thyme
- 1 large chopped onion
- 2 tablespoons chopped garlic

METHOD

1. In a large soup pot or Dutch oven add meat, cassareep and cover with water.
2. Cook for 45 minutes or until meat is somewhat tender.
3. Add the rest of the ingredients and simmer for another hour until meat is tender.
4. Adjust seasoning with salt and sugar.
5. Serve with roti, rice or bread and butter.

*HOW TO MAKE CASSAREEP

INGREDIENTS

- 4-5 cassava root
- 1 cinnamon stick
- 5 teaspoons brown sugar
- 1 teaspoon ground cloves
- Pinch salt

METHOD

1. Peel, wash and grate cassava root.
2. Place a cup of shredded cassava in a cheesecloth or clean kitchen towel.
3. Squeeze juice into a pot to extract the liquid
4. Boil for at least 45 minutes until it is reduced by half to a thick consistency, like molasses.
5. Flavour with spices, sugar and salt to taste.

SERVES 8

CREAM OF PUMPKIN

INGREDIENTS

2 pounds pumpkin or butternut squash, peeled and diced

1 large onion, diced

½ clove garlic

4 tablespoons chicken soup base (or bouillon cubes)

3 litres of chicken stock or water

2 tablespoons of fresh thyme, chopped

Salt and pepper to taste

½ cup of flour

1 tablespoon fresh ginger, grated

METHOD

1. In a large stock pot, add chicken stock or water, cover and bring to a boil.
2. Add pumpkin, onions, garlic, thyme and soup base.
3. Cook for ½ hour.
4. Remove the pumpkin and puree in a food processor, careful not to burn yourself.
5. Return to stock whisking vigorously to smooth.
6. Season with salt and pepper to taste.
7. In a small bowl add flour with ½ cup water, whisk into a paste.
8. Add to soup for a creamy consistency.
9. Serve with whipped cream (optional).

Serves 8

Bar Specials

Between the Sheet
Rough Rider
Big Bamboo
Elli's Bommer
White Witch
Planter Punch
Rum Punch
Fruit Punch
Tom Collins
Vodka Collins
Yellow Bird
Humming Bird

Homestyle Beverages

Wikipedia describes water as a chemical substance with the formula H_2O Its molecule contains one oxygen and two hydrogen atoms. Water is the most essential element to life on Earth!

What Does H_2O Mean To You?

Why am I talking about H_2O? I did a cooking demo with Adam Giambrone, former Chair for TTC. Danielle, our photographer, offered him bottled water. His reaction stunned me. "I would much prefer tap water," he said. Being a local celebrity, I assumed he couldn't drink anything but Evian, Perrier etc. Having been blessed to work around celebrities from all walks of life, I get to see how finicky they get about their favourite beverage.

As a kid growing up, my mother used to do some shopping in Haiti and Caracas. What I remember most about her trip was not what she brought back for us, but what she took; Mom always brought her own boiled water. I often thought back then, "Poor people, they don't even have water to drink!"

Today I am a big connoisseur of the H_2O. It's my favourite beverage. I drink it morning, noon and night consuming 10 to 12 glasses per day. I drink it bottled, tap, mineral, hot, cold and yes, Grace Coconut Water! I am always tempted to try the local water whenever I travel. Water tastes different! From developed countries, Third World regions to small towns.

Mr. Giambrone claims tap water is more vigorously tested; less chance of being contaminated. As a politician, he should know. Which brings us to the question; do you care about your water consumption, quality, and safety or how our actions affect the future generations?

As a teenager, one of my experiments was trying to turn sea water into fresh water; let's just say it involved electricity, some fuse blowing and my Mom not too happy. Reflecting on this topic I now realize that being a water bearer (Aquarius, sign of the zodiac), I am destined to like all things water. When I am agitated, need inspiration or even to pray for guidance, my solace is to find a large body of water. It not only nourishes me but feeds my soul, body and mind.

In this section, the base for all the homestyle beverages is water—highlighting its great versatility.

Cheers!

CARIBBEAN RUM PUNCH

INGREDIENTS

1 cup fresh lime juice

1 cup grenadine

1 cup simple syrup

3 cups amber rum

4 cups orange juice

4 dashes bitters

METHOD

1. In a pitcher, combine lime juice, simple syrup, rum and orange juice.
2. Add a few dashes of bitters.
3. Serve chilled over ice.

SERVES 4

CINNAMON CRANBERRY CHRISTMAS TEA

There's nothing like a warm cup of tea to liven up the Christmas celebration. This cinnamon-laced cranberry tea has a bit of citrus to give it a little spark. Place the tea in a crock pot, on low temperature, to keep it warm and tasty all day long.

INGREDIENTS

4 quarts of water

1½ cups of sugar

6 cinnamon sticks

8 cups of cranberry juice

4 cups of orange juice

⅓ cup of lemon juice

METHOD

1. Pour the water into a medium-large pot and place it over high heat.
2. Add the sugar and cinnamon and bring the mixture to boil.
3. Reduce the heat to low, cover the pan and simmer for 25 minutes.
4. Remove the cinnamon sticks and discard.
5. Pour the cranberry juice, orange juice and lemon juice into the mixture and stir to blend them in well.
6. Serve warm with a cinnamon stick in each cup.

Makes 32 servings.

GOLDEN CHRISTMAS PUNCH

This pretty and tasty punch will be a perfect addition to your Christmas buffet table. Pineapple rings may also be added to the ring mold if you like.

INGREDIENTS

- 4 maraschino cherries
- 1 orange, sliced thin
- 1 lemon, sliced thin
- 1 lime, sliced thin
- 2¾ cups of water, divided
- 1 (12 ounce) can frozen lemonade concentrate, thawed
- 1 (12 ounce) can frozen limeade concentrate, thawed
- 1 (12 ounce) can frozen pineapple orange concentrate, thawed
- 2 litres ginger ale, chilled

METHOD

1. Place the cherries, orange slices, lemon slices and lime slices into a ring mold.
2. Pour the water into the mold and freeze until solid.
3. Pour the remaining water into a punch bowl.
4. Stir in the lemonade, limeade and pineapple orange concentrates until well blended.
5. Pour the ginger ale into the punch.
6. Unmold the fruit ice ring and place fruit side up into the punch.

MAKES 21 SERVINGS.

Our recipe winner, Nadine Spencer, from The Best Island Rum Punch Recipe Contest.

NADINE'S SPICED RUM PUNCH COCKTAIL
WHICH IN THE WINTER
TURNS TO A DELICIOUS HOT RUM TODDY

I love this cocktail year round and in the winter I warm all ingredients together on the stove for a Winter Warm Rum Hot Toddy —NADINE SPENCER

INGREDIENTS

    1 cup orange juice

    2 ounces dark rum (Appleton is my favourite)

    1 tablespoon Pimento Liquer

    4 clove sticks

    1 slice lemon

    1 cinnamon stick

METHOD

1. In a cocktail shaker, with ice, add all the ingredients
2. Shake well
3. Pour into cocktail glass with ice

Garnish with lemon and cinnamon stick

ADDITIONAL INGREDIENTS FOR WINTER

    ½ cup orange juice

    ½ cup water

    1 teaspoon honey

    4 clove sticks

METHOD IN WINTER

1. In a pot bring ½ cup water to a boil and add ½ cup orange juice
2. Add all ingredients in a small pot
3. Add 1 teaspoon honey
4. Add 4 clove sticks
5. Bring to a slight simmer

Serve into a glass mug with lemon and cinnamon stick

Delicious!

SORREL DRINK

No Caribbean Christmas would be complete without a cold refreshing glass of Sorrel.

INGREDIENTS

1 cup dried sorrel petals

1 cup sliced ginger

1 tablespoon cloves

A piece of dried orange peel

Brown sugar syrup (1 cup water + 1 pound brown sugar, boiled together)

Dark rum or sherry wine, optional

METHOD

1. Boil 2 quarts of water.
2. Once water is boiling, add sorrel, ginger, orange peel and cloves.
3. Boil for 30 minutes.
4. Cover tightly and steep overnight.
5. Strain and add sugar syrup and rum/sherry wine (optional) to taste.
6. Chill and serve.

Makes 8 servings.

There's nothing more comforting than curling up in front of a warm fire with a good cup of hot chocolate or mulled cider. Warm beverages have a way of taking the bluster out of a cold winter day. The ideas for a warm beverage are endless. Here are just a few suggestions to get you started on that cup of warmth.

A Cup of Warmth
to Brighten a Cold Winter's Day

HOT CHOCOLATE

Kids and adults savour the taste of hot chocolate. Warm milk, chocolate and marshmallows have a way of soothing us. Today packaged hot chocolate mix is in abundance. There are numerous types and various flavours. Yet there's nothing quite like homemade hot chocolate to warm and soothe a cold and tired body.

MULLED CIDER

Apple cider is a great way to warm up on a blustery day. Mulled cider gets its comforting effect from spices infused in the flavour during heating. Cinnamon, nutmeg and cloves are the spices most often used. Mace, ginger, allspice, orange slices and lemon zest can also bring out the flavour of a mulled cider. It's best to use whole spices to achieve a full flavour. Ground spices may be used, but the taste will differ slightly.

For best results when making mulled cider, steep the cider over low heat. Simmering the cider for a couple of hours will bring out the best flavour. Do not boil the cider or the taste may become bitter. To keep your cider warm, place it in a crock pot after simmering.

HOT TEA

We are fast finding in today's world that tea is one drink that offers a healthy alternative to caffeinated drinks. An abundance of flavoured teas, comforting teas and healthy teas are available in supermarkets everywhere.

Herbal teas have also become more popular. Most herbal teas contain no caffeine. Spearmint tea is soothing and is easy on the digestive system. Peppermint tea is also quite soothing but can be hard on the bladder and digestive system if consumed on a regular basis. Mint teas also have large amounts of vitamin C. This may also be a problem for those whose bodies are sensitive to this vitamin. Regulate your mint intake in teas by making your own. Add mint leaves to tea while steeping. It may take a few tries to find the right adjustment of mint, but it is well worth it when it when you do find the perfect dose.

Chamomile tea is another comforting herbal tea. Chamomile is great for naturally relieving muscle spasms that can be brought on by the cold weather. Be careful if you are allergic to ragweed as chamomile is related to the ragweed family.

FLAVOURED HOT WATER

This beverage might sound a little strange but with some imagination flavoured hot waters can be quite delicious. Add flavoured extracts with a tiny bit of brown sugar or honey. Stir in orange, lemon or lime zest to add flavour. Spices can be added to give hot water a delicious taste.

These are just a few ideas on how to achieve a soothing cup of warmth.
Experiment with different herbs and spices or head off
to the supermarket to see what is available.

Relax and enjoy.

Winters Abroad

When the days are short and the weather is frigid, we look for foods that are comforting. Often times these foods will soothe the soul, but they won't warm the toes. Luckily, there are certain foods you can eat to help warm up your body temperature.

Foods Perfect for Warming Up On Cold Winter Days

There are also foods that should be avoided if you're looking to warm yourself up on the inside and out. We'll talk a bit about both.

FOODS THAT WARM THE BODY

Adding certain foods to your diet on a daily basis can make a difference in your body temperature. Some of these items may not come as a surprise to you, but others may have you asking yourself if they really do make a difference?

NUTS & SEEDS

Peanuts and almonds are easy to incorporate into a diet. 10 soaked almonds or a handful of peanuts can give the body deep warmth that lasts.

Seeds such as sesame, pumpkin and fennel are great body warmers. Sesame seeds can be incorporated into many dishes, such as green beans or chicken. Pumpkin seeds are great as a snack when roasted. Fennel seeds can also be added to foods. These seeds are great for the digestive system and help to warm the body no matter how you choose to use them.

SPICES & MORE

Cinnamon, cloves, ginger and pepper are warming spices. Ground cinnamon can be added to add flavour to many of our baked foods. Cinnamon sticks give a wonderful taste to many warm beverages, such as tea.

Cloves are not only warming but they are a great mouth freshener. Because they have antiseptic properties, they not only help with bad breath, but can also keep other parts of your body healthy. Ginger can be added to soups or vegetables to help incorporate this spice into our daily diets.

Pepper just yells out warmth. Sprinkle a little pepper onto your foods in place of the extra salt.

Honey is effective when it comes to warming the body. Honey is a natural sweetener that can be added to just about anything sugar is used in. Honey is also great for the complexion.

Onions and garlic are easy to incorporate into most meals. These little gems not only help in keeping the body warm but can also be helpful in keeping the body healthy. Have a cold? Try a little garlic to open up those stuffy noses. Lowering cholesterol is also one of the benefits of garlic and onions.

FRUITS & VEGGIES

Fruits and vegetables will also give the body the warmth it needs. Add a serving of fruits and vegetables to each of your meals every single day. It's just what the doctor ordered. We all know fruits and vegetables are healthy, but when added to your daily diet in the winter time, they help to warm your entire body by boosting your immune system, blood flow and much more.

FOODS TO AVOID IN WINTER

Not all foods are the greatest if warmth is what you're after. There are some foods that should be avoided in order to stay toasty in the winter. First things first, remember not to overeat on a cold winter night. Overeating can jump start your metabolism which burns off the extra calories needed to keep the body warm. It can also extinguish digestive fires which help in fending off the chill.

Certain foods that should be avoided include:
* White breads
* Cucumbers
* Too much butter
* Cold drinks
* Rice (especially at night)
* Alcohol
* Processed chips

These foods can also heighten metabolism and add to your blustery feeling.

These are just a few of the foods to eat and to avoid during those cold winter months. The next time you curl up in front of the TV with a warm blanket to fight off the winter chill, try snacking on a few of the foods listed above to help keep you warm. You might be surprised at how well it works.

LEMON HOT PEPPER SHRIMP

These shrimp will make the perfect appetizers. Serve in the sauce with a slotted spoon and lemon slices on the side.

INGREDIENTS

- 1 pound butter
- 3 lemons, sliced
- 3 tablespoons of pepper
- ½ teaspoon of salt
- 2 cloves of garlic, minced
- 2 tablespoons of Worcestershire sauce
- ½ teaspoon of hot pepper sauce
- 2½ pounds shrimp, uncooked in shells

METHOD

1. Set the oven temperature to 375ºF and preheat.
2. Place the butter into a large saucepan and place on medium heat.
3. Let the butter completely melt & add the lemon slices.
4. Stir in the pepper, salt and garlic.
5. Pour in the Worcestershire sauce and hot pepper sauce and blend in well.
6. Bring the mixture to a gentle boil.
7. Reduce the heat to low, cover the pan and simmer 30 minutes, stirring often.
8. Lay the shrimp into the bottom of a large roasting pan.
9. Pour the simmered sauce over the shrimp.
10. Bake 20 minutes or until the shrimp turn pink.

MAKES 12 SERVINGS

GINGERED PORK STEW

Tender cubes of pork are cooked in a blend of soy sauce, sherry, scallions, garlic, sugar and ginger to make this tasty dish.

INGREDIENTS

- 1 pound boneless pork loin, cubed
- 2 cloves of garlic, mashed
- 1 tablespoon grated fresh root ginger
- 2 tablespoons sherry
- 1 tablespoon soy sauce
- 1 teaspoon sugar
- 3 tablespoons peanut oil
- 1 red bell pepper, julienned
- 1 yellow bell pepper, julienned
- 1 bunch scallions, sliced
- ½ cup chicken stock
- 2 teaspoons cornstarch

METHOD

1. Place cubed pork in a dish and mix with the garlic, ginger and a dash of salt and pepper. Cover with plastic wrap and let marinate for 30 minutes.
2. Blend together the stock, sherry, soy sauce, sugar and cornstarch in a bowl.
3. Heat oil in a wok or large frying pan, add pork and stir fry for 3 minutes.
4. Add peppers and scallion, stir fry for another 2 minutes.
5. Add soy sauce mixture, stir and bring to a boil. Lower the heat, cover and simmer for 15 minutes.
6. Check occasionally to make sure sauce is not thickening too much. If needed, add water.

Just close your eyes and picture yourself in Grandma's kitchen. Can you smell those fresh baked cookies or those scrumptious pies? Just the thought of baking gives anyone that warm to the toes feeling. Baking doesn't have to be a culinary art. It's simple, fun and can make a cold winter chill vanish in a blink of an eye.

Baking Essentials for a Warm Day in the Kitchen

When Grandma baked, it was usually from scratch. No box mixes or canned pie filling could be found in her pantry. In today's hustle and bustle world, a pre-packaged mix brings a quick reality to most kitchens. There's nothing wrong with that, but a day of scratch baking can also bring a little relief from a stressful life.

Baking is not really an art. The hardest part of baking is making sure you have all the essentials needed. This list is a good place to start when checking for items that are necessary to turn the kitchen into a baker's delight.

FLOUR
All-purpose flour is a must but depending on what you are baking you may also need self-rising flour, wheat flour or millet flour. Just be careful not to substitute in a recipe. Flours consist of different properties and can make or break the easiest of recipes.

SUGAR
White and brown sugars are a must when baking. Brown sugar can be found in light or dark. Light brown sugar usually works best when baking because it gives those baked goods a delicious flavour. Use dark brown sugar when the recipe calls for it.

BUTTER OR MARGARINE
Which is better? In most cases one can be substituted for the other, but if a recipe calls for butter specifically, do not substitute margarine. Regular butter will give your recipe more flavour and when used sparingly won't cause as many health problems. Sweet, unsalted butter is best because the salt can mask the flavour of food. Be careful with salted butter because it masks the smell and taste of the butter which means it could easily go rancid without your knowledge.

COOKING OILS & SPRAYS

When it comes to baking, oils rank at the top of important items to have on hand. They help to make our baked items moist and tasty. Non-stick cooking sprays make greasing those pans easier and more economical.

BAKING POWDER & BAKING SODA

These leavening agents are important leavening ingredients in order for your baked items to rise during the baking process.

EGGS & DAIRY PRODUCTS

Eggs are the "glue" that hold your baked goods together. They are also a large part of the rising process. Most recipes will call for large eggs and these are the best bet for consistent results. Dairy products like milk and creams are a staple in many baking recipes as well.

SPICES

These can make or break a recipe. Spices add flavour to those baked goods. Be sure to add only spices that will give the flavour you need. Apple pie spice, pumpkin pie spice and other specialized spices include many different spices combined saving you both time and money.

BAKEWARE & COOKING UTENSILS

Measuring cups and measuring spoons are very important to ensure you add just the right amount of ingredients to batters. A whisk, pastry blender and rubber spatulas are also necessary in preparing those batters. An electric mixer, blender or food processor can help in cutting down preparation times.

Cookie sheets, cake pans, muffin tins, pie pans and brownie pans are all necessary when baking. Cake pans come in round or rectangular shape and in all different sizes. Brownie pans are usually square and come in 8 or 9-inch sizes. Depending on just how in-depth you want to take your baking, you may also need tube pans, spring form pans or Bundt pans.

Baking is a simple pleasure that anyone can enjoy. Baking is a great way to introduce children to the kitchen too. It is definitely a way to make your home feel warm and cozy when it's cold outside. Take the chill off and bake a batch of cookies or a loaf of bread this afternoon.

CARIBBEAN COCONUT MACAROONS

This is a favourite treat in the Spanish speaking islands. Here's is a simple recipe.

INGREDIENTS

> 2¾ cups coconut flakes
>
> ½ cup flour
>
> 4 egg yolks
>
> 1 cup brown sugar
>
> ¼ cup butter
>
> 3 tablespoons coconut (or vanilla) extract

METHOD

1. Preheat oven to 350ºF.
2. Grease a 13-inch cookie sheet.
3. In a bowl, thoroughly mix all ingredients together to form a dough.
4. Divide the dough into 24 pieces and form into balls.
5. Place the balls on the greased cookie sheet and bake for 20 to 25 minutes until golden brown.

SERVINGS: 24 COOKIES

SELWYN'S TIP

Add nuts or drizzle with chocolate sauce

Spices play an important part in making delicious meals. They give our foods distinct flavour and aroma. Winter spices can give your body warmth. Here are just a few that can help steer off that 'down to the bone' chill that winter so graciously offers.

Winter Spices to Help Fight a Chill and More

CINNAMON. This winter spice is used often for its distinctive taste and smell. Add a cinnamon stick to a hot beverage. Ground cinnamon is a great topping for toast, oatmeal and fruit. Cinnamon also finds its way into baked foods, chili and soup. Cinnamon can be used as a natural sweetener for applesauce. Diabetics can use this winter spice to help reduce blood sugar levels along with triglycerides and cholesterol.

GINGER. Ginger not only warms a cold body, but is also quite healthy. This spice is known for having powerful anti-inflammatory agents. Many use this spice to help with migraine headaches, arthritis and nausea. Ginger can be added to soups, to top vegetables or sprinkled over meats to give them a tangy flavour. It can also give tea a zesty kick.

CLOVES. Cloves have a unique taste. They are often used when roasting meats to give the meat a robust flavour. Hams are especially tasty when topped with cloves. This spice can be used in teas or baked foods. Cloves are also known for their anti-inflammatory properties.

TURMERIC. This Indian spice is usually found in powder form. It adds flavour to soups, stews and chili. It can be used when roasting meats and is often found in pasta sauce. Scientific studies have shown that turmeric not only warms the body but can also help in protecting the body against cancer. Turmeric has been used for treating stomach ulcers and relieving free radical stress in people suffering inflammation.

CARDAMOM. In experimental studies, cardamom has been shown to prevent cancer and help in detoxifying the liver. Cardamom is often used in conjunction with cinnamon. Teas, ciders and flavoured hot waters are enhanced by cardamom. Cardamom can also be used when flavouring foods with cloves to enhance the flavours and aroma.

PEPPER. Just the sound of pepper warms a body. Pepper is a strong spice often used when cooking bland dishes. This spice gives a pungent flavour to almost any food. Adding a little extra pepper instead of salt to your foods can be both a warming and healthy benefit. Pepper is also said to be helpful to those who have asthma.

These are just a few of the winter spices that will help head off that cold winter chill. Add them to any of your favourite foods. The taste and smell are sure to warm the body and comfort the soul.

HOT JAMAICAN CHOCOLATE TEA

This traditional hot chocolate drink is a comforting addition to winters abroad. Nothing brings back the taste and smell of your childhood like some good old 'chocklit' tea. Jamaican chocolate tea should not be confused with store-bought hot chocolate. The chocolate we are referring to is the seed from the cocoa pods which are removed, dried roasted and grounded into manageable golf size balls or pucks.

INGREDIENTS

    1 Jamaican chocolate ball, grated

    ½ cup condensed milk

    6 cups water

    1 cinnamon stick or 1 teaspoon ground cinnamon

    ½ teaspoon salt

METHOD

1. Bring water to boil in a medium pot and then add grated chocolate (cocoa) and cinnamon.
2. Boil for another 15 minutes then sweeten with condensed milk and salt.
3. Strain into cups and be careful to sip, because of the oil content of the chocolate it retains heat for a long time.
4. Enjoy!

Serves 4 - 6

SELWYN'S TIP

Chocolate balls can be found at any West Indian store or International market

Sometimes when it's cold, and snowy outside, the comfort of a good home cooked meal is all you need to warm up. Meat and potatoes have a way of making us feel good and helping us ward off those cold winter days. For many, a roast may seem too scary to attempt but in reality it's as simple as making a sandwich.

Let the Comfort of a Good Roast Warm You

THE ART OF COOKING

Large tender cuts of beef, pork and lamb make the best roasts. When purchasing a roast, look for marbling or flecks of fat within the lean meat. This marbling increases the juiciness of the meat giving it more flavours along with making these cuts more tender. Aged beef will also enhance the roast's flavour.

When it comes to types of meats to roast, there are many to choose from. Turkeys and hams are often roasted to enhance their flavour. Beef roasts and pork roasts are favourites, but roasted prime rib and leg of lamb are mighty tasty too. Even a roasted chicken can be juicer and have more flavour than fried chicken.

TIPS FOR TURNING OUT THE PERFECT ROAST

When roasting a cut of meat, be sure it is at least 2- inches thick. This will guarantee a moister and less chewy dish. Moist heat is important when roasting a large cut of meat. A large cut of meat when slow cooked should be braised to ensure a mouth-watering and juicy finished product.

Browning the meat is a plus. It doesn't matter if you are slow cooking on top of the stove, in the crock pot or in the oven, browning meat before hand over high heat will help to caramelize the proteins and sugars found on the outside of the meat. This gives your roast a richer flavour.

It is best to season a roast before browning it. By doing this prior to browning, the flavours are sealed into the meat and not left in the bottom of a roasting pan. Roasts are best cooked at 300°F.

If you are using vegetables such as potatoes, carrots, onions and celery and using a crock pot, always add the vegetables at the beginning of the cooking process. You want your vegetables to be soft so let them cook longer at the slow temperature.

If you are adding vegetables to a roast in the oven, add them about one hour before the roast has finished cooking. They will be soft instead of mushy from being overcooked or crunchy from not being cooked enough.

Liquids can also be added to roasts. Water, broths, soups, juices, wine and even soda can be added to help keep your roast juicy and flavourful. Always be sure to cover your pan with foil or a tight lid to keep the liquids from escaping and causing your roast to become too dry.

One last tip—remember a meat thermometer. Different meats cook in different time spans. A meat thermometer is the most reliable way to tell when any meat product is cooked all the way through.

Roasts make the best 'fix it and forget it' meals. Add a side of fruit and a slice of warm homemade bread and you have a meal that is both comforting and warming.

WINTER ROAST MADE EASY

INGREDIENTS

2 tablespoons unsalted butter

1 tablespoon sunflower oil

1 large onion, cut into wedges

3 pound boneless top round or rump roast

3 carrots, peeled and thinly sliced

3 medium white potatoes, cubed

2 bay leaves

½ teaspoon salt

2 envelopes onion soup mix

1 tablespoon cornstarch

METHOD

1. Over medium heat, melt butter in the sunflower oil.
2. Place the beef and onion wedges in the hot oil.
3. Brown the beef but only brown each side. Meat will cook through in crock pot.
4. Once meat is browned, place meat and onions in the crock pot.
5. Add carrots, potatoes and bay leaves. Add salt.
6. Mix onion soup mix in 3 cups of boiling water until completely dissolved.
7. Pour over top of the meat and vegetables.
8. Cook on high about 3½ hours or until meat is fork tender.
9. To make the gravy, place cornstarch and 1 teaspoon of water in a medium saucepan.
10. Stir until mixture becomes a paste.
11. Add 2 cups of liquid from meat.
12. Boil until liquid thickens into desired consistency.

SERVES 6 - 8

Salad Days

There aren't a lot of foods that can hold more than one place on the food pyramid. But, long before we started talking about super foods, ancient peoples knew the benefits this humble food had to offer; as a vegetable, a protein, and a healer.

The Humble Bean.
A Super Food Leading a Double Life

In traditional Indian medicine, there exists an age-old system of living and healing that includes a vegetarian diet using legumes like lentils, beans, and peas to keep the body healthy. Now, beyond the Middle-Eastern cultures, many people recognize the power of the bean to support whole nutrition and well-being. Here, we discuss some of the benefits of beans, and why they are leading a double life as a well-respected super food.

PERFECT NUTRITION ON MANY LEVELS

Legumes are edible seeds contained in pods, and beans are part of that family. By their very nature, beans have a convenience factor that makes them a favourite food in many parts of the world including the Caribbean islands. They are generally inexpensive and store well with the potential for a long shelf life, particularly when they are dried. Beans offer sustained nutrition and energy due to the fact they have a low glycemic index, meaning they provide energy to the body over a long period of time.

You won't get bored quickly eating beans, either. There is virtually an endless variety of beans and legumes to choose from, as well as a mountain of recipes to try when adding beans to your healthy diet. A short list of beans would include navy beans, black beans, lentils, soybeans, great northern beans, mung beans, garbanzo beans, pinto beans, black eyed peas, and kidney beans.

Beans are an excellent source of dietary fiber, minerals, and vitamins, and are naturally low in fat, calories, and sodium. You can serve beans in nutritious main dishes or side dishes that will satisfy your appetite with less-costly consequences to your body, or budget. These reasons alone would easily earn beans their super food status, but there's more!

Eating several servings of beans each day not only helps you reach your daily vegetable requirement, but those same beans also add up as your protein intake. Yes, those inexpensive, versatile beans are a protein. That's why we consider them a double-duty super food. Beans can easily be combined in recipes with other protein sources, vegetables, and starches like corn, whole wheat, or brown rice to create 'complete proteins' containing all the necessary amino acids our bodies require to function well.

GLORIOUS BROILED GARDEN TOMATO BASIL SALAD

INGREDIENTS

4 large sweet beefsteak tomatoes

Olive oil

½ teaspoon kosher salt

¼ teaspoon freshly ground black pepper

¼ cup fresh basil, coarse chopped

8 fresh baby mozzarella balls, cut into small pieces

4 strips bacon, diced and crisp fried, drained

METHOD

1. Wash and cut the tomatoes in half across the 'equator' and carefully cut out the insides, chop up and put in a bowl.
2. Add to the bowl with the tomato pulp, the kosher salt, black pepper, basil, and mozzarella balls pieces. Mix to combine.
3. Place each tomato 'bowl' cut side up on a broiler pan and brush lightly with olive oil.
4. With slotted spoon, fill the bowls with the tomato-basil-mozzarella mixture, making sure you don't get too much tomato juice in the tomato bowl.
5. Place under preheated broiler at 5-inches away for about 3 to 4 minutes or until tops brown, tomato softens, and cheese is melted.
6. Remove and let cool slightly.
7. Sprinkle crumbled bacon on top and serve warm.

MAKES 8 INDIVIDUAL SALAD SERVINGS

LIMA AND BUTTER BEAN SALAD

You can add or change the type of beans used in this recipe. For example, try kidney beans, black eyed peas or more for a 3-bean or 5-bean salad. Get creative!

INGREDIENTS

2 (15¼ ounce) cans lima beans, drained
2 (15 ounce) cans butter beans, drained
2 sweet red peppers, chopped
2 green peppers, chopped
1 large sweet onion, chopped
4 garlic cloves, minced
½ cup of lemon juice
½ cup of olive oil
4 tablespoons of cider vinegar
1 teaspoon ground cumin
½ teaspoon pepper
2 teaspoons Grace All Purpose Seasoning

METHOD

1. Place both types of beans into a serving bowl and toss to combine.
2. Add the red peppers, green peppers, onion and garlic and toss again.
3. In a small mixing bowl whisk together the lemon juice, oil and vinegar.
4. Add the cumin and pepper and whisk until blended in well.
5. Pour the mixture over the bean mixture and toss to coat well.
6. Cover with plastic wrap and chill for at least 1 hour before serving.

MAKES 8 SERVINGS

When new gardeners start plotting out their garden, typically the first harvest they envision is the tomato. Yes, the good old tomato ranks first among all the vegetables we imagine in our dream gardens. Why is that? Because the garden tomato is not only easy to grow, but freshly picked, is the tastiest of all vegetables.

Turn the Humble Garden Tomato into a Gourmet Salad Star

Tomatoes have often been thought of as the 'blue collar' vegetable - good, but not gourmet. But even a good old fashioned tomato can produce culinary brilliance when treated with a little imagination.

A LITTLE BACKGROUND

The tomato wasn't always so beloved or accepted. At one point, the tomato was considered suspect, even poison. However, as the tomato traveled from South America, to Central America, to North America, and then into Europe, this fruit (yes, the tomato is a fruit) kept gaining favour.

This unsuspecting treat started out as a tiny, gnarly, even wild fruit. Growers have been developing hybrid tomatoes ever since, creating bigger, smoother crops. However, during this hybrid process, we've lost much of the flavour of the true tomato.

Growing your own tomatoes can help you get back to the basics; a sweet, firm, flavourful tomato. Once you get closer to the tomatoes that the Aztecs worshiped, you'll enjoy flavours that will have you singing the praises of tomatoes as a gourmet treat.

AN OLD FASHIONED FAVOURITE TAKES CENTRE STAGE

Tomatoes are one of the more versatile veggies in the garden. It's difficult to think of tomatoes as gourmet, but it's time to rethink. When you plant a tomato, you expect a fresh salad at harvest time, but perhaps you haven't given a gourmet salad much thought. Most likely you've thought of the tomato as an addition to a green salad. It's time to give fresh tomatoes a bigger stage on the family table.

Yes, tomatoes give a glorious boost to mixed greens in a salad. But, as a central ingredient in salads, you can't go wrong with the bright colours and flavours of the garden grown tomato. There are so many ways to turn this simple side show into a headliner.

TOMATO AND MOZZARELLA CHEESE WITH BALSAMIC VINAIGRETTE AND PEA SPROUTS

When choosing tomato plants or tomatoes at your farmer's market, choose heirloom tomatoes or home-style, not hybrid, tomatoes for the best of both worlds. These tomatoes don't look like the tomatoes you may be used to in the produce aisles, but the further you get away from hybrids, the better the flavour.

Simple ideas for fresh tomatoes can produce gourmet classics. For instance, combine fresh diced tomatoes with prosciutto, baby mozzarella, fresh basil, and a drizzle of balsamic vinaigrette or even just a good olive oil, and you'll discover a salad that is bound to please even the most jaded gourmet. Or skip all the other ingredients and cut up a variety of tomatoes of all shapes, colours, sizes, and flavours for a surprising salad that's both simple and elegant. Splash with a mix of good olive oil and balsamic vinegar, a dash of kosher salt, and your choice of herbs to give the tomato a chance to really stand out.

Another option is to use fresh tomatoes as a bowl or 'vehicle' for a crab salad, tuna salad, shrimp salad, smoked salmon, or other main-dish style salad for a special luncheon or light dinner. Scoop the inside out of a large, sweet tomato, dice and combine with other fresh veggies, then fill the tomato 'bowl' and serve.

You can serve a hot salad with the same basic ideas. Sauté onions and mushrooms, then toss with chopped kale and dill, put inside the tomato bowl, top with shredded provolone or mozzarella cheese and set under the broiler just long enough to melt the cheese. Now you have a wonderful hot salad, side dish, or luncheon favourite with unexpected flavours.

There is no end to the excitement a fresh garden tomato can elicit when combined with other imaginative flavours or when standing on its own fresh good taste. The gourmet happens when you get creative and think way beyond the notion that a tomato is just a supporting actor in your salad. Make it the star and taste the possibilities!

GOURMET RADICCHIO SALAD IN ROASTED ACORN RINGS

INGREDIENTS

1 small acorn squash

Olive oil

Kosher salt for baking

1 pound Portobello mushrooms, washed

1 head radicchio, shredded

1 cup baby arugula

1 Granny Smith apple, unpeeled, cored, and diced, then sprinkled with a dash of red wine vinegar

3 tablespoons pumpkin seeds

3 tablespoons red wine vinegar

1 tablespoon olive oil

Kosher salt

METHOD

1. Preheat oven to 375°F.
2. Scrub the acorn squash and cut into ½-inch thick rings.
3. Remove seeds and pulp from each ring.
4. Put rings in large bowl and drizzle olive oil in bowl
5. Sprinkle with kosher salt
6. Lay out on baking sheet and roast for 15 to 20 minutes or until the squash is tender and starting to brown nicely.
7. Do the same with the Portobello mushrooms.
8. Once both the acorn rings and Portobello mushrooms are roasted and removed from oven, start arranging the salad.
9. In a large bowl, toss the radicchio, arugula, prepared apple, and pumpkin seeds, then add the red wine vinegar, olive oil, and salt, tossing again lightly to coat well.
10. To assemble the salad, put an acorn squash ring on a salad plate and place a serving of the salad inside the ring.
11. Cut the Portobello mushrooms into thin wedges and arrange them around the salad.
12. Drizzle completed salads with more vinegar and oil if desired.

SERVES 4 - 6

CUCUMBER SALAD

INGREDIENTS

1 small cucumber

½ teaspoon sugar

3 teaspoons lime juice

Dash of rum

3 tablespoons olive oil

2 spring onions, sliced

METHOD

1. Deseed cucumber and cut into julienne.

2. Add sugar, lime juice, rum, oil and spring onions.

3. Toss well.

Serve with Green Fig (green bananas) and Saltfish recipe

SERVES 2 - 4

BERMUDA HORSESHOE BAY COURTESY BERMUDA TOURIST BOARD.

If you enjoy making fruit salads as part of your summer fare during picnics and family get-togethers, you're going to love the suggestions we have for you here. Knowing how to combine the right blend of fruits in a salad, either alone or with other ingredients, is the first step to creating fruit salads that impress and delight your guests.

Create Dazzling Delicious Gourmet Fresh Fruit Salads

COMBINE INGREDIENTS THAT COMPLIMENT

Certain fruits are better candidates for a combination of greens and fruit salad, but that doesn't mean you can't experiment a little to find new flavours you enjoy. Summer melons like honeydew and cantaloupe are always good, but a number of different fruits and berries are equally compatible with some basic greens such as romaine lettuce or other mixed varieties. Consider adding, for instance, grapefruit segments to add zip and zing to an otherwise traditional spinach salad. It's all about the flavours playing off each other.

If it's just fruit in the salad you're making, the sky's the limit as to what you might combine for a delicious treat with your meals. Lots of different berries are in season in the warmer months, so consider adding two or three different varieties to a more basic fruit salad made with bananas, apples, and grapes. A little splash of freshly squeezed lemon juice will help keep everything fresh.

Stick with a light dressing, like a vinaigrette that's not too strong or too sweet. This will allow the tartness and sweetness of the strawberries, mango, peaches, cranberries, or whatever you use to come through in the salad. And, don't forget the texture. Adding some roasted almonds adds a bit of crunch and depth in flavour to this type of salad creation. The salty flavour of the nuts also compliment the sweetness of the fruit. Using opposing flavours will often 'marry' the ingredients together, creating a perfectly blended compliment of flavours.

CREATE INTEREST WITH ONE OR TWO SURPRISING INGREDIENTS

You only need a slice or two of an exotic, unusual fruit to create excitement in a salad. Star fruit, dragon fruit, dates, mandarin segments, apricots, figs, and papaya are just some suggestions, and they don't have to be considered a dessert salad either. Combining one or two of these fancy fruits in a mixed green salad, chicken salad, tuna salad, shrimp salad, crab salad, or meat based salad could create quite a buzz at your next dinner.

Remember, there's also a selection of spices and herbs that do wonders to perk up a fruit salad. And don't just think about sweet spices like cinnamon, ginger, nutmeg, cloves, and allspice. Mixing hot pepper flakes or chili powder with sweet ingredients often is the perfect compliment. Savoury herbs like rosemary, dill, and thyme are also surprising when used to enhance fruit salads.

WHEN PRESENTATION MATTERS THE MOST

Special occasions may call for a salad that looks as good as it tastes. This is where you employ additional ingredients and combine colours and layers to make a presentation and a statement with your delicious creation.

Use a melon baller, for instance, to scoop up delicate pieces of the melons you choose. Then, include layers of colour with blueberries, blackberries, sliced cherries, or raspberries. Garnish your fruit salad with lemon balm or mint leaves for extra colour. Other fruit favourites include fresh pineapple, kiwi, or tangerine slices. Think about shapes, sizes, and colour, then mix and match for a salad that looks as good as it tastes.

Mixing fresh fruit with creamy layers of vanilla pudding is another pretty salad to serve guests for a special dinner party. Add a little whipped cream and a maraschino cherry on top for a final touch. A similar look is possible by mixing cream cheese and condensed milk together for the base that holds your favourite fresh fruits.

Drain your fruits well before combining them, then you can even make a gourmet version of the old fashioned fruit salads found on holiday tables many years ago. Make it gourmet by using crème fraiche (a thick cream that is slightly sour), and lots of fresh fruit, including berries, and even roasted nuts.

These suggestions are just a quick look at the possibilities for making gourmet fruit salads using your imagination and good taste. Having a healthy appetite for adventure will spur on the type of creativity you'll need to make splendid fruit salads that are an unexpected pleasure.

MARINATED BERRIES ON FRESH BABY SPINACH

1 pint ripe strawberries, hulled and sliced

1 pint ripe blueberries, washed and dried

2 tablespoons red wine vinegar

1 tablespoon light olive oil

1 tablespoon light brown sugar

1 teaspoon poppy seeds

1 tablespoon minced shallot

⅛ teaspoon smoky paprika

¼ teaspoon kosher salt

12 ounce baby spinach

Chopped walnuts

Bleu cheese crumbles

METHOD

1. Clean strawberries and blueberries and put in large bowl.
2. Whisk together in a separate bowl the vinegar, olive oil, sugar, poppy seeds, shallot, paprika, and salt, until frothy - then pour over berries.
3. Let berries marinate for 30 minutes, stirring frequently.
4. Divide spinach between individual salad bowls.
5. Spoon marinated berries over the top of each salad, then top with a sprinkling of walnuts and bleu cheese crumbles.
6. Serve immediately.

SERVES 4

Chef's Classics

Foods to Help with Your Iron Intake

It is recommended that females between the ages 11-50 years consume about 50 mg of iron per day; it is even higher for pregnant women, between 30 - 60mg per day. Surrounded by a lot of lovely women, I can't help but hear their complaints about low iron, feeling lethargic and unmotivated. Iron deficiency is a condition where a person has an inadequate amount of iron to meet the body's demands. It is a decrease in the amount of red cells in the blood caused by having too little iron.

The highest source of iron usually comes from animal products e.g. liver and red meat. Many women will not include liver as part of their diet or will only eat meat that is cooked well done. I suggest that you start ordering your steak medium and stop cooking your liver like shoe leather. Chicken livers are great for making pate, a nice hors d'oeuvre that is simple to make. Some foods when eaten raw provide iron that is absorbed more efficiently. So tomorrow for lunch why not order the spinach salad with a sprinkle of sliced almonds or how about that five-bean salad?

Cooking spinach: start with onions, portabella mushroom some diced tomatoes, seasonings, adding spinach for the last two minutes. Next time you're in the grocery store grab some collard greens, add green cabbage, red wine vinegar, seasoning and a dash of sugar. It takes getting used to but watch your energy levels go up. Start experimenting with all the foods that your mom told you were good for you, but you thought were yucky!

Ok! How about juicing your spinach with carrots, apples or cucumbers? You get the idea! Let your imagination be your guide. You don't like green bananas? Treat them like they were mashed potatoes with parmesan cheese.

Look at ways to improve your iron diet, and just maybe you will not have to take a needle from your doctor to address your iron deficiency.

COURTESY JAMAICA TOURIST BOARD

PAN FRY LIVER WITH SAUTÉED ONIONS

INGREDIENTS

1 pound sliced calf liver

1 large onion, sliced

Salt and pepper

1 cup all-purpose flour

1 teaspoon chopped fresh thyme

½ cup vegetable oil

METHOD

1. In a shallow dish add flour, salt and pepper or a bit of meat seasoning.
2. Dredge sliced liver (not cubed) in flour.
3. In a medium frying pan add vegetable oil.
4. On medium heat add liver, 2 minutes per side.
5. Remove from pan and set aside.
6. In a small frying pan add 2 teaspoons of vegetable oil.
7. On medium heat add sliced onions, sauté to golden brown (careful not to burn).
8. Add salt and pepper to taste with chopped thyme.
9. Place on top of liver; reheat in oven a couple minutes before serving.
10. Great with sautéed spinach and green mashed bananas.

SERVES 4

SELWYN'S TIP

For a super successful liver and onions dish that will turn around any liver hater:

i) Soak the liver in milk first for 30 minutes or so

(ii) Don't manipulate the liver too much while it's cooking—turn only once

(iii) Cook for no more than two minutes per side or it will become leathery

PENNE PASTA WITH BABY VEGETABLES

INGREDIENTS

- 3 cups package penne or rigatoni
- 3 large tomatoes, chopped
- 1 small onion, chopped
- 1 garlic clove, chopped
- 1 cup tomato-based pasta sauce
- 3 cups assorted diced vegetables, fresh or frozen or fresh spinach
- 3 basil leaves fresh, chopped or pinch dried
- 1 tablespoon oregano
- 2 tablespoons parmesan cheese
- 2 tablespoons olive oil

METHOD

1. In a large sauce pan add water and bring to a boil.
2. Add pasta and cook al dente 8 to 10 minutes.
3. Meanwhile, in a wide saucepan over medium heat, add olive oil, chopped onions and garlic, stirring often.
4. Cook for about 3 minutes then add tomatoes, basil and oregano.
5. Add fresh vegetables 2 minutes before pasta is cooked.
6. Drain well, add to sauce, stir well and sprinkle with parmesan cheese.

ST. LUCIAN GREEN FIG (GREEN BANANAS) AND SALTFISH

INGREDIENTS

½ pound salt cod filet

Coconut oil or olive oil for frying

1 small onion, chopped

1 tablespoon chilies, chopped

1 clove garlic, chopped

2 spring onions, sliced

3 medium tomatoes, diced

2 green bananas boiled until tender, cut into quarters

1½ tablespoons mayonnaise

Hot pepper sauce to taste

Sprig coriander and parsley chopped

METHOD

1. Prepare the salted cod by rinsing off excess salt.
2. Put in a pot and cover with cold water.
3. Bring to boil, then drain.
4. Repeat 2 to 3 times until water is no longer salty.
5. Flake the filet.
6. Heat oil in large frying pan.
7. Sauté onions, garlic and peppers.
8. Add spring onions, stir well.
9. Remove from heat and add flaked saltfish, tomatoes and hot pepper sauce.
10. Finally, add bananas and mayonnaise to bind.
11. Serve sprinkled with fresh herbs.

SERVES 4

Serve with cucumber salad recipe

RASTA PASTA

Jamaica has the highest population of Rastafarians, their bright colours of red, green and gold are ever present. The following recipe mimics the Rastafarian colours and highlights their vegetarian cuisine. Many do not use salt in their diet.

INGREDIENTS

  3 cups fresh tri-colour tortellini

  3 cups assorted diced fresh vegetables

  3 large tomatoes, chopped

  1 medium onion, chopped

  1 clove of garlic, chopped

  1 cup tomato base pasta sauce

  ½ coconut milk (optional)

  1 tablespoon fresh thyme, chopped

  1 tablespoon fresh basil, chopped

  1 tablespoon oregano

  3 tablespoons olive oil

  2 tablespoons parmesan cheese

  Salt and pepper to taste

METHOD

1. Bring a large pot of lightly salted water to a boil, add 1 tablespoon of olive oil and cook tortellini for 8 minutes or until al dente.

2. Meanwhile, in a wide saucepan over medium heat add the rest of olive oil, sauté onions and garlic, stirring often so as not to burn.

3. Cook for about 3 minutes then add tomatoes, thyme, oregano, coconut milk and pasta sauce.

4. Add fresh vegetables to pasta (two minutes before pasta is cooked).

5. Drain pasta well, add to sauce, add basil, stir well and sprinkle with parmesan cheese.

Sample Menus

Easter Parade of Flavours

Bermudan Codfish Cakes

Glorious Broiled Garden Tomato Basil Salad

Honey Glazed Ham with Pineapple Relish & Mixed Berries

Mango Cheesecake

Caribbean Rum Punch (with or without the rum)

Hot Coffee and Tea

SELWYN'S TIP

Decorate table with Easter tablecloth, napkins and utensils.
Add a decorated Easter egg to each place setting

Christmas with a Rum-po-po-pum

Cream of Pumpkin Soup

Gourmet Radicchio Salad in Roasted Acorn Rings

Perfect Holiday Turkey

Escoveitch of Red Snapper Filets

Jamaican Rice and Peas

Penne Pasta with Vegetables

Classic Caribbean Christmas Rum Cake

Sorrel Drink with Rum

Hot Coffee and Cinnamon Cranberry Christmas Tea

SELWYN'S TIP

Decorate table with Christmas tablecloth, napkins and utensils.
Add a small, brightly wrapped gift to each place setting as a favour. Play Christmas music

Backyard Cook-out

Conch Fritters

Fresh Garden Salad

BBQ Pork with Jerk Marinade and Tamarind Chutney

Island Burgers with Grilled Pineapple Salsa

BBQ Chicken

Festival Dumplings

Jamaican Rice and Peas

A Little Different Apple Pie-a-la Mode

COURTESY JAMAICA TOURIST BOARD

Lyming or Hanging Out

An Informal Relaxing Environment

Jamaican or Guyanese Pepperpot Soup

Ackee & Smoked Salmon Val-Au-Vent

Boneless Jerk Chicken

Bakes or Festival

Banana Bread

Caribbean Rum Punch

Selwyn Richards, born and raised in Jamaica, has been planning and cooking delicious food with artistic flare for over 25 years. He studied Culinary Management at George Brown College in Toronto and started his culinary career as a Kitchen Manager with Culture's Food Service. He worked in a variety of prestigious restaurants in and around Toronto working with the Skyline Hotel, The Island Yacht Club, the prestigious Top Of Toronto Restaurant at the CN Tower as a Sous Chef, The Earl Of Whitchurch-Stouffville and was part of the opening team for SkyDome where he headed his own department as Head Chef.

Selwyn's broad experience in the Hospitality and Food Services industries, coupled with a talent and enthusiasm for restaurant excellence, resulted in Selwyn owning and managing his own upscale Caribbean restaurant and catering company with his brothers Lennox and Travis. Traveling all over the Caribbean, North America and Europe, their company received a number of write-ups from local newspapers and appearances on City TV's "Breakfast Television", CTV Canada AM, and CBC TV. He was also Chef for the Jamaican 50th celebrations in Canada.

It has been said that Selwyn creates a feast for the eyes as well as the palate! At the Food & Wine Show in 1987 (sponsored by the Escofier Society of Toronto), Selwyn was recognized for achieving these high standards of excellence in the culinary arts and was awarded two silver medals and one bronze.

Below is a list of film and TV productions that Selwyn has contributed his Food Styling expertise to in the last few years:

Alphas	Comfort & Joy	Nikita
American Pie 5: The Naked Mile	Copper	Poe
Anonymous Rex	Covert Affairs	Suburban Madness
Beautiful People	Defiance	Suits
Blizzard	Dresden Files	Take This Waltz
Bomb Girls	Fever Pitch	The Bridge
Breakout Kings	Home Again	The Strain
Carrie	Horizon	Unnatural History
Cheaper By The Dozen 2	Just Visiting	

Recognized as an expert in his field, Selwyn and his company, The Art of Catering, are renowned for their TV appearances on such shows as I Do... Let's Eat! (Food Network), Rich Bride, Poor Bride (Life Network) and Soul Food (BET Network/Showtime). Interviews and live radio broadcasts with Selwyn have been heard on G98.7 Fm, Irie Fm Jamaica CIUT 89.5 FM, AM 640 and CHRY 105.5 FM in Toronto and WBLK 93.7 FM in Buffalo. Selwyn is a contributor to publications such as *Planet Africa* magazine, *Wisdom*, *Pride, Extra*, and *Share* newspaper featuring his articles and recipes.

Many refer to Grace as the *"Food from the Caribbean"*. For people from the Caribbean islands, it's the *"taste of home"*, an icon which symbolizes premium quality, trust and respect.

GraceKennedy Limited.
Taking the Taste of the Caribbean
to the World

The story of GraceKennedy goes back to 1922, when Dr. John J. Grace and Mr. Fred William Kennedy founded the organization in Kingston, Jamaica on Valentine's Day as a small trading establishment. Founded on the pillars of honesty, integrity and trust, today GraceKennedy has expanded into a network of some 60 subsidiaries and associated companies employing over 2,500 people in the Caribbean, North and Central America, Europe, Asia and Africa.

Our mission, in part, is "To take the taste of Jamaican and other Caribbean foods to the world." GraceKennedy prides itself on offering consumers the flavour and goodness of the islands and its product portfolio ranges from Coconut Water, Hot Sauces, an exotic juice range fondly known as Tropical Rhythm, Island Soda, Corned Beef, Chicken Vienna, and Coconut products such as Coconut Milk, Coconut Oil, Coconut Water and Coconut Sugar, just to name a few. In total, the Grace brand offers over 2000 food products all born and inspired in the Islands and packaged with care and love "Island Style".

Grace food products are now available in many supermarkets, ethnic and exotic food stores across USA, Canada, UK, Africa and the Caribbean which speaks volumes of the trust that people of various nationalities have placed in the brand.

Operating on the principle that the success of the company is inextricably linked to that of the society in which it operates, GraceKennedy has contributed generously to various areas of national development throughout the years. In addition to providing financial assistance to a host of worthy

causes, GraceKennedy has institutionalised its programme of support through its two Foundations. These are the GraceKennedy Foundation, which focuses on giving assistance in the area of education, and the Grace and Staff Community Development Foundation which offers assistance to inner city communities. The Company's subsidiaries based outside of Jamaica are also actively involved in giving back to communities wherever they are located.

In addition to marketing and distributing its own brands, GraceKennedy Companies overseas represent other popular Caribbean brands in our quest to bring Caribbean foods to the world.

As an organization which prides itself on connecting with its customers, we invite you to visit any of our social media platforms to get to know us better, learn about our products, new offerings, discover recipes created with Grace products or even share the recipe of your favourite Caribbean dish for others to enjoy. We are a few keystrokes away and love to hear from you.

As the leading Caribbean food company, GraceKennedy wishes to thank Chef Selwyn Richards for his tireless dedication to bringing the best of the Caribbean by showcasing its culinary delights to the world. We are also grateful for the opportunity to support his labour of love through his book, *The Art of Cooking: Soul of the Caribbean.*